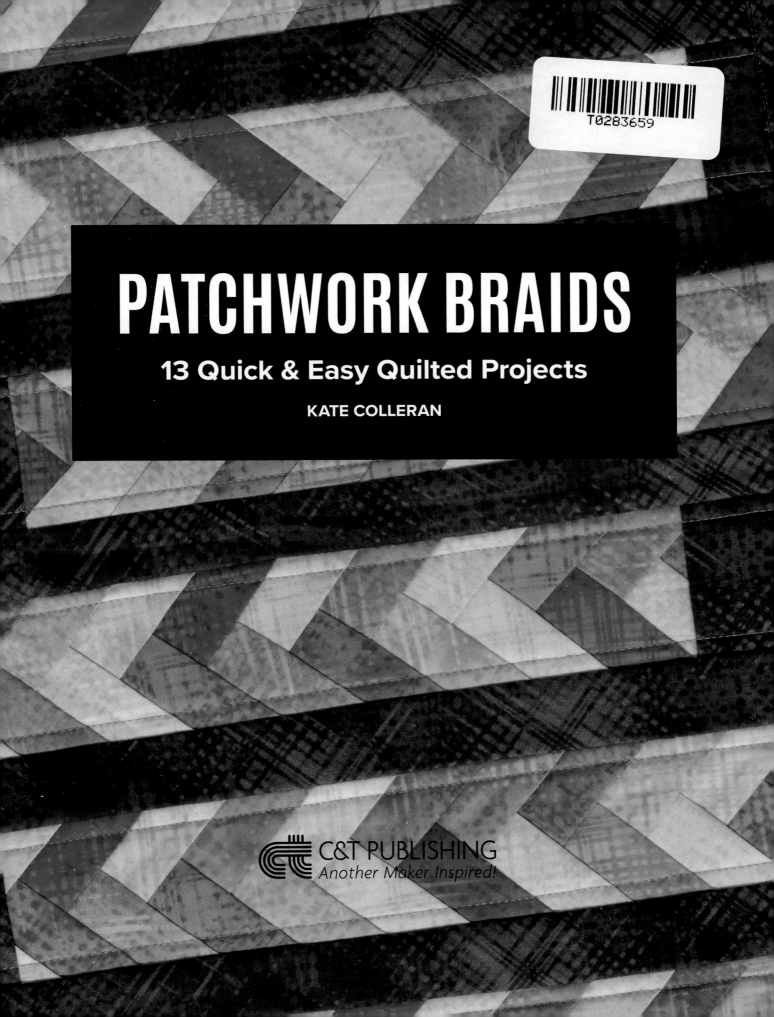

PATCHWORK BRAIDS

13 Quick & Easy Quilted Projects

KATE COLLERAN

C&T PUBLISHING
Another Maker Inspired!

Text copyright © 2025 by Kate Colleran

Photography and artwork copyright © 2025 by C&T Publishing, Inc.

Publisher: Amy Barrett-Daffin

Creative Director: Gailen Runge

Senior Editor: Roxane Cerda

Technical Editor: Helen Frost

Cover/Book Designer: April Mostek

Production Coordinator: Zinnia Heinzmann

Illustrator: Kirstie L. Petterson

Photography Coordinator: Rachel Ackley

Front cover photography by Kate Colleran

Subjects photography by C&T Publishing; lifestyle photography by Jodi Foucher; instructional photography by Kate Colleran unless otherwise noted

Published by C&T Publishing, Inc., P.O. Box 1456, Lafayette, CA 94549

Library of Congress Cataloging-in-Publication Data

Names: Colleran, Kate Carlson, 1959- author.

Title: Patchwork braids : 13 quick & easy quilted projects / Kate Colleran.

Description: Lafayette, CA : C&T Publishing, [2025] | Summary: "Learn a quick and easy method to piece braids and how to alter them to add a new creative layer to your quilts. Once you know the concept, you can design your own braid projects or make one of the thirteen projects included inside to show off your new skills"-- Provided by publisher.

Identifiers: LCCN 2024030781 | ISBN 9781644035603 (trade paperback) | ISBN 9781644035610 (ebook)

Subjects: LCSH: Patchwork. | Patchwork quilts. | Patchwork--Patterns. | Quilting--Patterns. | BISAC: CRAFTS & HOBBIES / Patchwork | CRAFTS & HOBBIES / Sewing

Classification: LCC TT835 .C64725 2025 | DDC 746.46/041--dc23/eng/20240711

LC record available at https://lccn.loc.gov/2024030781

Printed in China

10 9 8 7 6 5 4 3 2 1

DEDICATION

To my friend and quilting buddy Crystal Zagnoli. You were sunshine, a bright spot in a cloudy day, a great friend, and the best long arm quilter anyone could ask for! You helped to make my business possible. I miss you but I am glad you are at peace. I hope you are wrapped in the love of all those whose lives you touched and made better by just being you.

ACKNOWLEDGMENTS

A big, huge, ginormous thank you to my husband, Jim, who is so supportive of me and my quilt business. I couldn't do it without you.

A shout-out to my daughter, Alyssa DesRosier, who is always willing to listen to me talk quilting and who gives great color and style advice. Thank you!

To Lisa Soderberg of The Quilted Cricket, who quilted so many of the projects in the book and did everything quickly and beautifully. Thank you!

To my quilting friends who listen, advise, and support: You're the best!

To all the staff at C&T Publishing, but especially to Roxane, who patiently answered my gazillion questions, thank you for all your support and guidance!

Thank you to Moda Fabrics, QT Fabrics, Robert Kaufman, Island Batik, Timeless Treasures, and The Warm Company, who provided fabric and batting for these fun braid projects!

To my sons Sean and Scott and my son- and daughters-in-law Rea, Jocelyn, and Jeff, thank you for your love and support. And to my furry quilt inspectors, Lark, Luna, and Kira, who got up close and personal with my quilts and gave the high paw of approval!

Contents

PROJECTS USING BASIC BRAIDS • 15

USING STRIPS OF VARYING SIZES IN YOUR BRAID • 32

INTRODUCTION

What is a braid quilt?

A braid quilt features blocks sewn from strips of fabric that, once pieced together and trimmed, look like woven strands—sort of like a long, braided ponytail! One version of a traditional braid quilt has long vertical braid blocks separated by sashings.

Braids can be scrappy, or they can use a coordinated fabric palette or fabric collection. The braid pieces are usually one piece of fabric, but they can be pieced strips combining different fabrics. Braids can also include squares placed along the center of the braid. You can achieve many different looks with a braid, and there are many different ways to piece a braid. It is a great technique to add to your quilter's toolbox!

Making a braid may seem hard, but it is a great technique for a beginner. I like to think of sewing a braid as Sunday afternoon sewing because you just add one piece at a time. It is not a race, and you don't have to match points; you grab one braid piece, sew, press, then add another braid piece, sew, press, and repeat. Making a braid is a relaxing, low-stress kind of sewing. You are just sewing straight lines, adding one piece at a time, and before you know it, you have a long, pieced strip that looks like it was hard to make!

Once you have a braid, it can be used in different ways in your projects. It can be the main block in a quilt, as in the *Blue Diamond Iris* quilt. It can be used as an accent, as in the *Plumeria* zipper pouch or the *Sapphire Tower* tote bag. Or it can be a supporting block, as in the *Clementine* quilt.

There are so many different ways to create and use your braid!

I *love* making braids; they are just *sew* much fun. I can't wait for you to get started!

Getting Started

GENERAL INFORMATION

I am so happy you are going on this journey into making braids with me! Let's start with some basic information. First, the book is written with the assumption that you have basic quilting supplies, including a rotary cutter, ruler, and mat, and that you know how to construct and bind a quilt.

Now, for some guidance on the patterns in this book!

• Seam allowances are built into the cutting instructions.

• All pieces are sewn with right sides together (RST) unless otherwise specified.

• Cutting instructions are based on 40″-wide fabric. Adjust fabric amounts and cutting as needed to fit your chosen fabrics.

• WOF means "width of fabric."

• I recommend following the arrows when pressing.

If you, like many quilters, sometimes need a refresher on a technique here and there, at the back of this book, you will find instructions for making Half-Square Triangles, Flying Geese, and swirling seams (see Basics Refresher, page 123).

SEAM ALLOWANCE

All the projects in this book use a ¼″ seam allowance. Braids have a **lot** of seams, so a seam allowance that is not a true ¼″ can change the size of the braid. The good news is that braids are very forgiving! For each project, you will make a braid and then trim the braid to the desired length. For most of the projects, I have built in some wiggle room so you can also trim a bit off from the sides.

You are most likely to notice a variation in your seam allowance in the length of your braid. If your seams are just slightly wider than ¼″, you may find that you need more braid pieces than listed in the pattern to be able to get the braid to be the size indicated. Conversely, if your seam allowance is a scant ¼″, you may need fewer pieces. Braids are flexible, and if you need more length, just cut a few extra pieces of fabric!

Some of the projects include pieced blocks, where your seam allowance will be even more important. To check your seam allowance, I suggest cutting two squares 2½″ × 2½″. Sew them together and press the seam to one side. Measure across the width; your piece should measure 4½″ wide. If it doesn't, it's time to adjust your seam allowance!

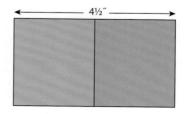

PRESSING

Pressing is critical when making braids. In most of the projects, I suggest pressing the seams to one side. You can follow the arrows for my pressing suggestions. Of course, if you prefer to press your seams open or have a different pressing plan in mind, you can do that too!

One thing to watch is **how** you press the braids. Braids are built on the bias, and therefore it is **really** easy to press them out of shape. In the past, I have managed to make a braid look like a C curve!

To press a braid, start with a dry iron. Using steam can stretch the fabric, which then stretches the braid out of shape. Press the seam flat and don't iron, which means don't move the iron all around the piece. Our instinct with a braid is to press toward the seam, but that is pressing toward an angle and can result in your braid starting to bend!

When making a braid, I like to gently finger-press each seam and sew a few braid pieces together before heading to the iron. With the iron, I press each seam flat from the right side of the braid and in the direction of the arrow. If I feel like I must move the iron, I move it gently up and down the length of the braid, not at an angle. Use the iron to help keep the braid straight!

BASIC BRAIDS

I made my first braid quilt for my book *Smash Your Precut Stash*. I designed it and then realized that I had never made a braid quilt before, so I asked a few quilting friends for advice and their thoughts on what they liked or didn't like about making a braid. The most common complaint was not knowing where to trim the sides of the braid.

There are many different ways to make a braid quilt. One way is to start with rectangles, but there is a bit of fabric waste when using rectangles, and it is often hard to know exactly where to trim the sides of your braid once the pieces are sewn together.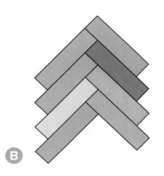

I like to start with the pieces for my braids already cut with one angled edge. Those angled edges form the sides of the braid, which makes it very easy to see where to trim the sides.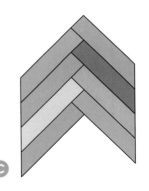

One drawback to sewing with the edge of the braid pieces cut on an angle is the sides of the braid are now on the bias. But if you start with rectangles, once you trim the braid, you will also have bias on the sides. To me, this is just something to be aware of and work with, not a problem.

For many of the projects in this book, you will cut the braid pieces with angled edges. For some, like the *Zinnia* table runner, you won't.

Size of the Braid

To start any braid, you first have to decide the size strips you want to use. Do you want to use wide 3″ strips, medium 2½″ or 2″ strips, or narrow 1″ strips? The smaller the width of the strip, the more braid pieces it will take to make the length of the braid. **D** – **E**

Next, you need to decide how wide you want your final braid to be. The wider the braid, the longer the braid piece you need.

I like to cut my pieces so my sewn braid is slightly wider than the size I need, because once it is sewn, I can trim just a bit off the sides and have a perfectly straight edge. I find that with all those seams that are in a braid, things can easily get a little wonky. Adding in some wiggle room is just a great idea!

The width of your braid is dependent on a couple of factors, the first being the length of the braid piece. For example, if you cut 2½″ strips into braid pieces 6″ long, your braid will be about 6⅜″ wide, and you can easily trim the braid to 6″ wide.

If you cut the 2½″ strips into braid pieces 7″ long, your braid will be about 7¾″ wide, and you can trim it to 7½″ or smaller. But the size is also determined by the width of the strip. If you cut 1¼″-wide strips into braid pieces 6½″ long, the braid will be about 8¾″ wide, while a braid with 2½″ strips cut into braid pieces 6½″ long will only be about 7″ wide.

Because your seam allowance is also a factor, the best way to figure out how long you need to cut your braid pieces is to do a test.

Let's walk through cutting and sewing a basic braid!

Cutting the Braid Pieces

All the projects in the book use a different size braid, and you are going to use templates to cut the pieces. I share two options for the templates. The first option is to use my acrylic templates. The Braid Template works for strips up to 3″ wide and can cut braid pieces from 5¾″ to 8½″ long. The Mini Braid Template works for strips up to 1½″ wide and can cut braid pieces from 3″ to 4″ long. I share a trick in the *Sunny Vale* sampler quilt on how to use the Mini Braid Template to cut a braid piece that is a little longer than the template!

The second option is to make your own templates by using the Template patterns (pages 125–127). To make your own templates, you need template plastic. Trace the template onto the template plastic with a pen or pencil; a fine permanent marker makes the best line. Cut out the template with scissors.

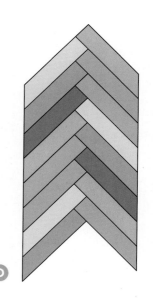

D

E

Cutting Fabric by Using Template Plastic

1. To start, cut a strip the desired width. Lay the fabric strip down, **folded in half, wrong sides together**. Trim off the selvedge end.

2. For the first cut, place the straight edge of template plastic along the cut edge of the fabric. Draw a line along the angled edge, remove the template, line up the mark with your ruler, and trim. **F**

CUTTING SAFETY TIP • Do not trim along the edge of your thin, plastic template with a rotary cutter. You will either trim off bits of the template or cut yourself. Always mark the line and then place a thick acrylic ruler on the line before cutting.

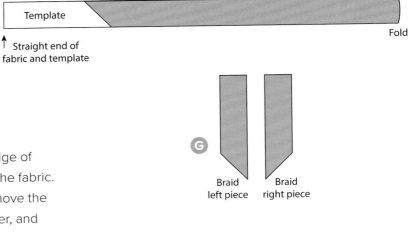

F Template · Fold · Straight end of fabric and template

G Braid left piece · Braid right piece

H Template · Fold · Angled end of fabric and template

Because your fabric is folded in half, you will now have 2 braid pieces with opposite angled edges. These will be the sides of your braid. *Note: If your strip is a single layer of fabric, all your braid pieces will have the same angle.* **G**

3. For the second cut, rotate the template and line up its angled edge with the angled cut edge of your fabric strip. Draw a line along the straight edge, remove the template, line up your ruler with the line, and cut. You will have 2 more braid pieces with opposite angled edges. Continue cutting along the strip. **H**

Cutting Fabric by Using the Braid Templates

1. If you're using a Braid Template, the process is similar. The difference is you can cut along the edge of the template. The templates also have lines you can use to cut different size braid pieces. To start, cut a strip the desired width. Lay the fabric strip down, **folded in half, wrong sides together**. Trim off the selvage end.

2. For the first cut, place the line for the size you are cutting along the cut edge of the fabric and cut along the angled edge. Note the edge of the template, where it says, "Line up along this edge." When cutting along the angled edge of the template, that should always be along the bottom edge of the fabric. *Note: For strips that are not as wide as the template, there will be space between the top of the strip and the top of the template.*

Because your fabric is folded in half, you will have 2 braid pieces with opposite angled edges. These will be the sides of your braid.

3. Rotate the template, but **don't turn it upside down**! Place the angled line for the size you are cutting along the angled cut edge of the fabric and cut along the straight edge. When the template is rotated to cut along the straight edge, the edge of the template where it says, "Line up along this edge" should always be along the top edge of the fabric. You will have 2 more braid pieces with opposite angled edges. Continue cutting along the strip. If you need additional guidance, refer to the handout that comes with the braid templates.

CUTTING TIP • If you are cutting your braid pieces and find that you have pieces of different sizes, it is probably because you did not line up the edge of the template that says "Line up along this edge" with the edge of the fabric; you used the other edge of the template! It is easy to do but will result in pieces that are smaller!

Sewing a Basic Braid

1. To sew a braid, you will start at the bottom of the braid. Line up a short straight edge of one left-side braid piece with the long edge of a right-side braid piece. Sew the short edge. Press toward the left piece. *Note: Sometimes quilters like to start their braid with a square. I only do that when I need that end of the braid to have a specific look or to be trimmed a specific way, such as in the Arrowleaf (page 56) or Pink Delight (page 64) quilts.*

2. Layer a left-side braid piece RST at the top of the braid, lining up straight edges. Sew. Press toward the new left-side braid piece. 🄹–🄻

3. Sew a right-side braid piece to the top of the braid, lining up straight edges. Press toward the right-side braid piece. Ⓜ

4. Keep adding pieces, alternating sides and pressing toward the piece just added.

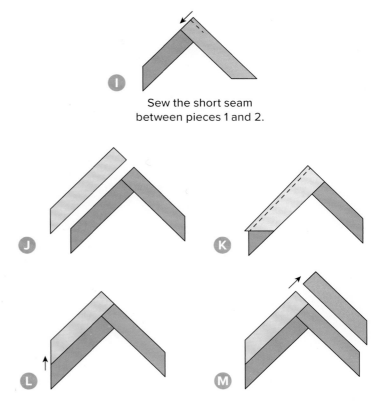

Sew the short seam between pieces 1 and 2.

TRIMMING A BASIC BRAID

1. To trim the braid, start at the bottom (beginning) of the braid. That way, if you discover that your braid isn't long enough, you can always add more pieces to the top end!

2. Trim across the bottom of the braid, above the intersection of the first two pieces. Then, measure up from the trimmed bottom edge of the braid to the desired length and trim across the top of the braid. Ⓝ

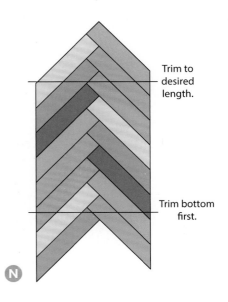

Trim to desired length.

Trim bottom first.

3. To trim the sides, trim approximately the same amount off each side so the braid is the desired width.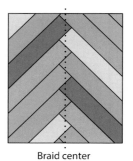

4. Braids that use varying sizes of strips, such as in the *Clementine* quilt (page 42), will have some longer pieces on the right edge. Let the pieces that are the same as the ones on the left side be your guide for how much to trim from the right side.

Trim even amounts off each side to the desired width.

TRIMMING TIP • The center of the braid is a little hard to find; it is between the top points of the braid pieces. You don't need to find the exact center to trim the sides. Eyeball it and trim about the same amount off each side. Unless you are really off-center, no one will be able to tell!

Braid center

COLOR AND MOVEMENT

Picking fabrics for your braid is so fun! Whether you decide to go scrappy, use a line of fabric, or work with a specific color palette, knowing how the colors work together will help the braid feel cohesive.

Color placement can help move your eyes along the braid. One thing to work on is making sure that strong colors have space between them and that they don't repeat on the same side too quickly. For example, if you use red in your braid, usually that is the first color you'll see, and if the red repeats quickly on one side of the braid, it will feel a little off. It's okay to use strong colors; you just want them to flow up and down the braid. **P**

When I am using a specific color scheme or group of fabric, I like to lay out the braid pieces before I sew them together. Each braid piece touches many other pieces, and I want to get a good flow of color and value. If all the dark pieces are lumped together, it can create sections so your eye seems to stop there and doesn't flow along the braid. **Q**

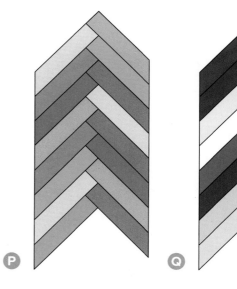

When you use an odd number of fabrics, and if you keep to a specific order for the braid pieces, the fabrics will naturally repeat in the same order, but on the other side of the braid. **R**

When you use an even number of fabrics, the fabrics will be on the opposite side, but not in the same order. **S**

Color and value are key to making the braid work. When we talked about trimming the braid, we mentioned that the center of the braid is between the top points of the braid pieces.

How can we change the **visual** center of the braid, or what we perceive as the center? To do that, add two pieces of the same color or value as a pair. **T**

You can see how that shifts what we perceive as the center of the braid! If you trimmed the braid with a similar amount off each side, the braid will look a little off-center. That's not always a bad thing! You can see that effect in the braids in the *Sapphire Tower* tote bag.

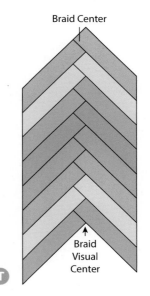

COLOR TIP • *If you are struggling with color placement, one tip is to step back from the braid. Distance can highlight value and color issues that you can't always see up close. One way to do that is to use a design wall. If you don't have a design wall, take a picture with your phone. A color photo will let you see what colors stand out, and a black-and-white or grayscale photo will show you value changes and highlight areas where colors are close in value.*

The bottom line is to play around with your braid pieces and with their order to find an arrangement you like!

HOW TO USE A BRAID

One way to use a braid is for it to be the main block in the quilt, such as in the *Blue Diamond Iris* quilt (page 20). It could also be cut into smaller blocks.

Other ways include using it as a border, as an accent, or as a motif, or even creating a block that isn't a braid but looks like one!

Border

A braid can be used as an inner or outer border in a quilt. In the *Sunny Vale* sampler quilt (page 96), the outer border is a braid. In the *Blue Dahlia* quilt (page 50), the braid is used as a partial border around a panel. Using a braid as a border around a panel can be done in a few different ways. In *Blue Dahlia*, the braid frames the panel but is also part of the outer border. For a different panel, another option might be to add a small braid around the panel and then create coordinating blocks to go around the inner panel section.

Motif

One motif that can be made with a braid is a tree. The angled edges lend themselves to looking like a tree block! In the *Pink Impression* quilt (page 88), I used the braid to create a flower block.

Faux Braid

The braid shape can also be created by piecing a block to give the impression of a braid without actually making a braid. The block in the *Daisy Chain* quilt (page 70) looks like a braid block with squares through the center. This magic happens by stitching and flipping some squares after the block is made to create the angled edges.

In this book, we are going to make a lot of different braids: basic braids with all the pieces the same size, braids where we add a square to the center of the braid, braids where we vary the size of the strips, and braids where we use pieced braid pieces.

As you work through the projects, you may notice they have all been named after flowers. I wanted each project in the book, and especially the sampler quilt, to feel bright and happy, like a garden of quilty goodness.

I am so excited! Let's start making braids.

PROJECTS USING BASIC BRAIDS

Now that you have learned how to make a basic braid, start making some fun and easy projects. If you have never made a braid before, this is a great place to begin!

The first project is a set of easy, quick, and practical placemats! For these, you will make a simple basic braid, cut it up, and sew the blocks into rows for your placemats.

The second project is a quilt that uses two sets of fabrics in two colorways to make two different braids. Sew them together with some sashing, and voila! You have a bold and dramatic quilt.

The third project is an easy zippered pouch where the braid is used as an accent. It adds some fun and flair to the outside of the bag, and small pouches are just so handy to corral your small quilting tools!

Alright ... let's make some braids!

BLUEBELL

Finished braid block: 2″ × 10″ • **Finished placemat:** 12½″ × 17½″

I love making placemats! They are a quick project and great for using that new line of fabric you just can't wait to play with or for using up your stash of leftover fabrics. Make them in various colorways to match the season or your mood. Placemats also make great gifts!

Fabric Selection

For the placemats, I chose to use an analogous colorway, which means I picked a few blues and a few greens; colors that are next to each other on the color wheel. This type of color scheme is harmonious and soothing. Most of the fabrics for the braid are a medium value, but with lots of color change. Because these are placemats, I wanted a slightly darker background, both to contrast with the braid and to mask crumbs!

Materials

Yardages are based on 40″-wide fabric. The fabric amounts listed will make two placemats.

Braid fabrics • ⅛ yard each of 9 different blue and green fabrics

Dark blue • ⅜ yard for background and setting

Binding • ⅜ yard

Backing • ⅞ yard

Batting • 2 pieces 20″ × 25″

BATTING TIP • A good batting to use in a placemat is thin or low loft. Warm and White from The Warm Company is a good option, as is fusible fleece.

Cutting

Braid Fabrics

From each of the 9 different fabrics, cut 2 strips 1¼″ × WOF. Using the Mini Braid Template or Template E (page 125), subcut into 26 braid pieces 1¼″ × 3″ from each fabric. If you need a refresher, refer to Cutting the Braid Pieces (page 9).

Dark Blue

Cut 4 strips 1½″ × WOF; subcut into 10 rectangles 1½″ × 12½″ and 8 rectangles 1½″ × 2½″.

Cut 1 strip 2½″ × WOF; subcut into 8 squares 2½″ × 2½″.

Binding

Cut 4 strips 2¼″ × WOF.

Backing

Cut 2 pieces 20″ × 25″.

MADE BY
Kate Colleran.

FABRICS ARE FROM
*the Vertex fabric line
from QT Fabrics.*

ASSEMBLY

Seam allowances are ¼″ unless otherwise noted. Follow the arrows for pressing suggestions.

Refer to instructions in Sewing a Basic Braid (page 11) and Trimming a Braid (page 11) as needed.

Making the Braids

1. Organize the fabrics into a pleasing arrangement. For my placemats, I arranged my braid pieces from light to dark first in the blues followed by the greens.

2. Sew the 1¼″ × 3″ braid pieces together into a long braid. You will need a braid approximately 130″ long.

3. Cut the braid into 12 rectangles 2½″ × 10½″.

CUTTING TIP • When making a really long braid that will be cut into smaller units, I like to cut as I go so I don't have to handle a lengthy braid piece. Once your braid is long enough, cut off your first rectangle from the bottom of the braid. Keep adding pieces to the top of the braid until you can cut the next rectangle and so on!

Cut 12 rectangles 2½″ × 10½″.

Making the Placemats

1. Sew a dark blue square 2½″ × 2½″ to the top end of a braid rectangle. Press toward the square. Column 1 should measure 2½″ × 12½″. Make 4 columns.

2. Sew a dark blue rectangle 1½″ × 2½″ to the top and bottom ends of a braid rectangle. Press toward the rectangles. Column 2 should measure 2½″ × 12½″. Make 4 columns.

3. Sew a dark blue square 2½″ × 2½″ to the bottom end of a braid rectangle. Press toward the square. Column 3 should measure 2½″ × 12½″. Make 4 columns.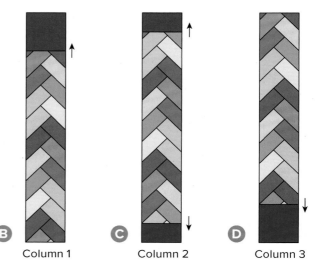

4. Arrange one of each column in order. Sew a dark blue rectangle 1½″ × 12½″ between the columns. Press toward the rectangles. Repeat to make 4 sections.

Column 1   Column 2   Column 3

Make 4 sections.

5. Sew a dark blue rectangle 1½″ × 12½″ between 2 sections, rotating the second section. Press toward the rectangle. Placemat top should measure 12½″ × 17½″. Make 2. **F**

Finishing

1. Layer each placemat top with batting and backing and quilt as desired.

2. Bind the placemats.

F

Make 2 placemat tops.

BLUE DIAMOND IRIS

Finished braid block: 8″ × 64″ • **Finished quilt:** 57¼″ × 67″

For this quilt, we are making long strips of braids with one colorway on one side and another colorway on the other side!

Fabric Selection

Iris is a two-color quilt. I needed to pick one color first so I could play off that color to choose the second color. I started with deep blue and then chose the complementary color of orange. Complimentary colors are ones that are on opposite sides of the color wheel. These color schemes are bold and dramatic!

For the blue side, I chose a selection of analogous blues, from aqua green to cerulean blue, in light to medium values. Then, for the oranges, I also chose a mix of analogous colors, from blue-red to yellow-orange, in the medium to dark value range. This method provided a nice complementary color scheme with some contrast of value between the two sides of the braid.

In each color group, I added a fabric that was at the outside edge of the palette. On the orange side, I sneaked in one raspberry color. It adds a pop of interest but doesn't take away from the rest of the braid. I didn't want to overmatch my braids and have them lose their liveliness!

Materials

Yardages are based on 40″-wide fabric.

Orange color fabrics: ½ yard each of 8 different fabrics for braid

Blue color fabrics: ½ yard each of 8 different fabrics for braid

Dark orange: ⅜ yard for sashing

Medium blue: ⅝ yard for sashing and border

Binding: ⅝ yard

Backing: 3¾ yards

Batting: 65″ × 75″

MADE BY
Kate Colleran, quilted by
Lisa Soderborg of The
Quilted Cricket.

FABRICS ARE FROM
*the Bella solids collection
from Moda Fabrics.*

Cutting

Orange Fabrics

From each of 8 different fabrics, cut 6 strips 2″ × WOF. Using the Braid Template or Template P (page 127), subcut 24 braid pieces 2″ × 7¾″ from each fabric. If you need a refresher, refer to Cutting the Braid Pieces (page 9). You'll need approximately 192 braid pieces.

Blue Color Fabrics

From each of 8 different fabrics, cut 6 strips 2″ × WOF. Using the Braid Template or Template P (page 127), subcut 24 braid pieces 2″ × 7¾″ from each fabric. You'll need approximately 192 braid pieces.

Dark Orange Sashing

Cut 6 strips 1¾″ × WOF; piece the ends together and subcut 3 sashing strips 1¾″ × 64½″.

Medium Blue Sashing and Border

Cut 10 strips 1¾″ × WOF; piece the ends together and subcut 2 sashing strips 1¾″ × 64½″, 2 side borders 1¾″ × 64½″, and 2 top and bottom borders 1¾″ × 57¼″.

Binding

Cut 7 strips 2¼″ × WOF.

Backing

Cut 2 pieces 65″ × WOF and piece crosswise to make a backing about 65″ wide × 75″ long.

ASSEMBLY

Seam allowances are ¼″ unless otherwise noted. Follow the arrows for pressing suggestions.

Braid Blocks

This quilt has six braids. Three braids are color group A, which has blue braid pieces on the left side and orange braid pieces on the right side. Three braids are color group B, which has orange braid pieces on the left side and blue braid pieces on the right side. Be sure to create three color group A braids and three color group B braids, or your quilt will look very different!

1. Separate the blue braid pieces into left and right piles. Then, separate the orange braid pieces into left and right piles. Put the left-side blue pieces together with the right-side orange pieces for color group A. Put the left-side orange pieces together with the right-side blue pieces for color group B.

Organize the colors in each group into a pleasing arrangement. I chose to follow the same color order of the blues and oranges for both color groups.

NOTE ON COLOR • I arranged the fabrics so there was a gradation of value and color. Some of my fabrics were very close in value or color to one another. You want to be careful about putting two fabrics that are similar in value next to each other, as they can sometimes form their own larger visual element and take over. You want the eye to travel up and down the braid, delighting in all the colors!

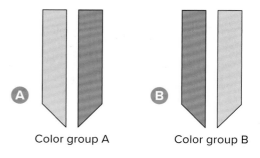

Color group A   Color group B

2. Refer to the instructions in Sewing a Basic Braid (page 11). Sew the color group A braid pieces together into a long braid. You will need a braid approximately 203″ long.

3. Trim into 3 long braids 8½″ × 64½″. If you need guidance, refer to Trimming a Basic Braid (page 11). **C**

CUTTING TIP • When making a really long braid that will be cut into smaller units, I like to cut as I go so I don't have to handle a lengthy braid piece—or in this case, a really, really long braid! Once your braid is long enough, cut off your first braid block, then keep adding pieces to the braid until you can cut the next one, and so on!

4. Repeat Steps 2 and 3, using the color group B braid pieces. **D**

MAKING THE QUILT

1. Refer to the quilt assembly diagram (page 24) and sew a color group A braid to the left side of a dark orange sashing 1¾″ × 64½″. Press toward the sashing.

2. Sew a color group B braid to the other side of the sashing. Press toward the sashing. Make 3 braid sections. **E**

3. Sew the sections together with a medium blue sashing 1¾″ × 64½″ between the sections. Press toward the sashing.

4. Sew a medium blue border 1¾″ × 64½″ to the side edges of the quilt top. Press toward the borders.

C Color group A braid

D Color group B braid

E Braid section

5. Sew a medium blue border 1¾˝ × 57¼˝ to the top and bottom of the quilt top. Press toward the borders. The quilt top should measure 57¼˝ wide × 67˝ long. **F**

FINISHING

1. Layer the quilt top with batting and backing and quilt as desired.

2. Bind the quilt.

F

Quilt assembly

PLUMERIA

Finished braid block: 2″ × 15″ • **Finished bag:** 11″ × 7½″ × 4″ deep

I love making bags, especially easy zipper bags that can hold all sorts of stuff. This one even has an optional inside pocket for more storage!

Fabric Selection

First, I chose the fabric for the outside of the bag. The main fabric is from the Gradients Auras collection by Moda. I used that fabric as a guide to pick all the other fabrics for the braid and the accent fabric. For those, I used an assortment of Bella Solids, Grunge Hits the Spot, and Essential Dots.

For the braid, I chose two fabrics, each in four different colors or color ranges: a medium and a light in blue, green, pink, and purple, then I added a medium orange paired with yellow. For the accent color, I used a solid purple.

Materials

Yardages are based on 40″-wide fabric.

Braid fabrics: ⅛ yard each of 10 different fabrics

Accent fabric: ⅛ yard

Bag fabric: ⅜ yard

Lining fabric: ⅜ yard

Fusible fleece: ⅜ yard

SF101 Shape-Flex or lightweight fusible interfacing: ¾ yard (based on 20″-wide interfacing)

16″ or longer nylon zipper

Cutting

Braid Fabrics

From each of 10 different fabrics, cut 1 strip 1″ × WOF. Using the Braid Template or Template B (page 125), subcut 5 braid pieces 1″ × 3″ from each fabric. If you need a refresher, refer to Cutting the Braid Pieces (page 9). You'll need approximately 50 braid pieces.

Accent Fabric

Cut 1 strip 1″ × WOF; subcut into 2 rectangles 1″ × 15½″.

Bag Fabric

Cut 1 strip 10″ × WOF; subcut into 2 rectangles 10″ × 15½″.

Subcut 1 rectangle into 1 rectangle 5½″ × 15½″, 1 rectangle 2″ × 15½″, and 1 rectangle 1½″ × 2½″.

Optional: For the inside pocket, cut 1 rectangle 10″ × 7½″.

Lining Fabric

Cut 1 strip 10″ × WOF; subcut into 2 rectangles 10″ × 15½″.

Fusible Fleece

Cut 2 rectangles 10″ × 15½″.

Shape-Flex

Cut 2 rectangles 10″ × 15½″.

Optional: For the inside pocket, cut 1 rectangle 5″ × 7½″.

1620
Mini-Braid
Template

KateColleranDesigns.com

©Kate Colleran 2016

Made in USA

1

3½   3

3   3½

line up along this edge

ASSEMBLY

Seam allowances are ¼″ unless otherwise noted. Follow the arrows for pressing suggestions.

Making the Braid

1. Organize the fabrics into a pleasing arrangement. For my braid, I arranged them in pairs by color and then alternated light and medium.

2. Refer to the instructions in Sewing a Basic Braid (page 11). Sew the 1″ × 3″ braid pieces together into a long braid. You will need a braid about 18″ long.

3. Trim the braid into 1 rectangle 2½″ × 15½″. If you need guidance, refer to Trimming a Basic Braid (page 11). Ⓐ

Bag Front and Back

1. Sew an accent fabric rectangle 1″ × 15½″ to the top and bottom of the braid rectangle. Press toward the accent rectangles.

2. Sew a bag fabric rectangle 2″ × 15½″ to the top of the braid unit and a bag fabric rectangle 5½″ × 15½″ to the bottom of the braid unit. Press toward the bag fabric rectangles. The front of the bag should measure 10″ × 15½″. Ⓑ

3. Layer the wrong side of the pieced bag front and the bag back rectangle 10″ × 15½″ with the fusible fleece rectangles 10″ × 15½″. Fuse the fleece to the bag pieces, following the manufacturer's instructions.

4. Quilt the bag front and back sections, if desired. I like to stitch ¼″ from the seam lines on the front of the bag.

Ⓐ

Trim to
2½″ × 15½″.

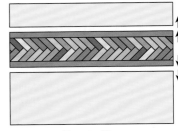

Ⓑ

Front of bag

Bag Lining and Optional Pocket

1. Layer the wrong side of the lining rectangles 10″ × 15½″ with the Shape-Flex rectangles 10″ × 15½″. Fuse the Shape-Flex to the lining pieces, following the manufacturer's instructions.

2. For the optional inside pocket, layer the Shape-Flex rectangle 5″ × 7½″ on one 7½″ edge on the wrong side of the pocket rectangle 10″ × 7½″. (The interfacing is used only on the top half of the pocket piece.) Fuse the Shape-Flex to the pocket piece, following the manufacturer's instructions.

3. Fold the pocket in half right sides together (RST) and sew the 2 side seams. 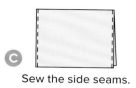 Ⓒ

4. Turn the pocket right side out. Turn under the lower edges ¼″ and press. Topstitch along the top folded edge of the pocket, approximately ⅛″ from the fold. Ⓓ

5. Center the pocket 2″ down from the top edge of a lining rectangle 10″ × 15½″ and topstitch along the sides and the bottom, approximately ⅛″ from the edges. This piece will be the back lining. Ⓔ

Preparing the Zipper

1. To make the zipper tab, fold the bag fabric rectangle 1½″ × 2½″ in half, wrong sides together, and press. Open and fold the edges to the center. Fold the piece in half and press again. The pressed piece should measure about ½″ wide. Ⓕ

2. At the top open end of the zipper, fold the zipper tape back at a 45-degree angle and baste in place. Ⓖ

3. With the zipper closed, measure the zipper to 14½″ long and trim the end.

4. Slip the trimmed end of the zipper into the zipper tab and topstitch across the tab to close and secure the end of the zipper. Trim the ends of the zipper tab even with the sides of the zipper. Ⓗ

Ⓒ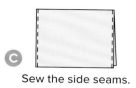
Sew the side seams.

Ⓓ
Fold ¼″

Turn under the lower edges ¼″ and topstitch along the top folded edge.

Ⓔ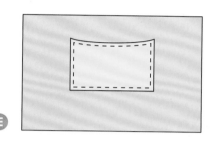

Ⓕ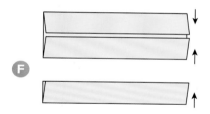

Ⓖ

Ⓗ

Bag

1. On the bottom 2 corners of all the bag and lining pieces, cut a square 2″ × 2″.

2. Layer the zipper right side up on the right side of the back lining piece. The tab end of the zipper should be ½″ from the right edge of the lining.

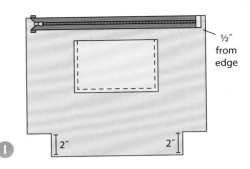

½″ from edge

2″   2″

3. Layer the bag back piece RST with the zipper and lining, matching up the sides, top, and bottom. Secure the layers with pins or binding clips.

SEWING TIP • If you are worried about the zipper moving between the layers when you go to sew, you can first baste the zipper to the top of the lining, using a ⅛″ seam. That way, it won't shift around when you add the bag piece.

4. With the zipper opened halfway, and using a zipper foot, sew across the top edge of the bag.

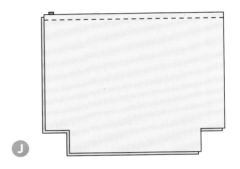

SEWING TIP • When you reach the zipper tab, with the needle in the down position through all the layers, reach underneath, close the zipper, and then finish sewing the seam.

5. Fold the bag piece back away from the zipper, and with the right side up, topstitch along the edge, approximately ⅛″ from the fold.

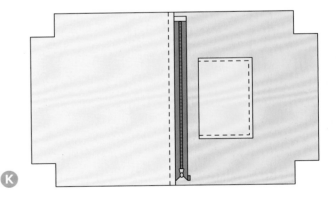

6. Fold the back lining away from the zipper. Layer the bag front RST with the bag back, matching the sides and with the top edge of the bag front even with the top edge of the zipper. Baste the zipper in place, if desired.

7. Layer the second lining piece RST with the back lining piece, matching the sides and with the top edge of the lining even with the top edge of the zipper. The zipper is sandwiched between the layers. Secure the layers with pins or binding clips. Note that the bottom edges will not line up with the previously sewn pieces.

8. With the zipper opened halfway, and using a zipper foot, sew across the top edge of the bag.

9. Fold the bag piece back away from the zipper, and with the right side up, topstitch along the edge, approximately ⅛″ from the fold.

10. Open the zipper most of the way. With RST, match the lining pieces together and the bag pieces together. Sew the side seams, keeping the zipper tab out of the seams.

11. Sew the bag bottom seam and the lining bottom seam, leaving a 6″ opening in the center for turning.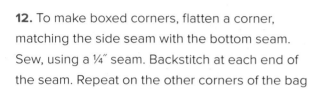

12. To make boxed corners, flatten a corner, matching the side seam with the bottom seam. Sew, using a ¼″ seam. Backstitch at each end of the seam. Repeat on the other corners of the bag and lining pieces. Ⓜ

PRESSING TIP • Press the side seam and the bottom seam in opposite directions so the seams nest together.

13. Turn the bag right sides out through the opening in the bottom of the lining. Fold in the raw edges on the opening in the lining, stitch closed, and then tuck the lining into the bag and push out the boxed corners. Ta-done!

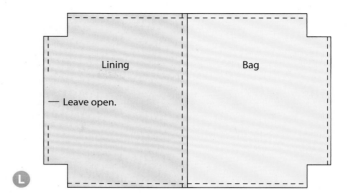

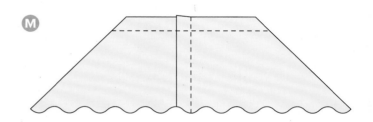

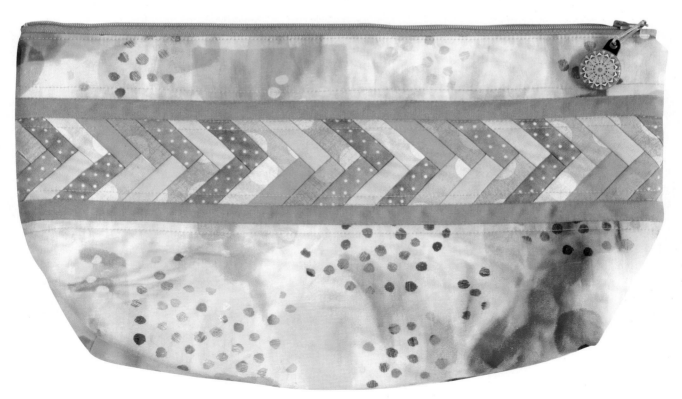

PLUMERIA

31

USING STRIPS OF VARYING SIZES IN YOUR BRAID

A fun way to mix up a braid is to vary the sizes of the strips used for the braid pieces!

Using strips of various widths for braids is easy; you can use just two different sizes, three sizes, or more! Just remember one thing as you add the braid pieces: Always add in pairs of braid pieces of the same size. The pieces don't need to be the same color or fabric (but they can be!)—they just need to be the same width.

In the *Blue Dahlia* quilt, I used a braid to frame a panel. The braid was made of pieces cut from strips of two different sizes. For this quilt, I cut two of the fabrics into braids using skinny strips, and for three colors, I cut the braids using slightly wider strips. When I sewed the braids together, I added pairs of the same size each time.

Detail shot of braid in *Blue Dahlia* quilt

In the *Clementine* quilt, I used four green fabrics and cut them into four different sizes! The dark skinny fabric strips were used in pairs between all the other colors to frame each one.

And in the tote bag, I used six different fabrics: five plaid fabrics and a coral linen that was cut into very skinny braid pieces. The coral was added between all the other fabrics. The other fabrics were all cut the same size and added in pairs, but not in pairs of the same color; I alternated the colors along the braid.

Detail shot of the braid in the *Sapphire Tower* tote

You have so many different ways to use varying size strips!

HOW TO USE VARYING SIZE BRAID PIECES

1. Cut your strips to the desired width and cut out your braid pieces all to the same length.

2. Lay out your pieces in a pleasing arrangement. Pieces 1 and 2 should be the same size. Then, the next 2 pieces should be the same size.

3. Continue to add strips, always in pairs that are the same size.

One thing you will notice is that as you build your braid, the pieces on the left side of the braid will line up, but the skinnier pieces will be longer on the right side. That is okay! We always trim the sides of the braid once it is pieced, so it will all even out then.

Why don't I cut the right-side skinny braids shorter? To be honest, I could. But usually I cut my braid pieces with the fabric strip folded in half, wrong sides together, so with each cut, I get a left and a right braid piece. To cut the braid pieces in different sizes, I would need to use a single layer and cut each one individually. And not having to worry about different sizes means the cutting goes faster!

When you trim the sides of your braid, ignore the longer skinny pieces on the right and trim using the wider pieces, that are the same as the ones on the left, as your guide. Let's make some braids with varying strip sizes! It's fun!

SAPPHIRE TOWER

Finished small braid blocks: 2″ × 6″ • **Finished long braid block:** 2″ × 14″
Finished bag: 12″ tall × 14″ wide × 4″ deep

Tote bags—you can never have too many! Especially ones with pockets, and this bag has lots of pockets: on the bag front and back, and on the inside!

Fabric Selection

I wanted my tote bag to have a dark color for the body of the bag and bright fabrics for the accent braids. The body of the bag is a Quilters Linen in a teal color called Peacock. I chose plaids from a line called Kitchen Window Wovens and then used another linen in coral for the accent color in the braid and another plaid in teal for the pocket linings. I love the pop of color of the bright plaids against the teal.

Materials

Yardage is based on 40″-wide fabric.

Braid fabrics: ⅛ yard each of 5 different plaid fabrics

Braid accent fabric: ⅛ yard

Bag fabric: 1⅛ yards

Pocket lining: ⅝ yard

Lining fabric: ¾ yard

Lightweight fusible interfacing: 2½ yards of 20″-wide interfacing

Heavyweight fusible interfacing, fusible fleece, or fusible foam: ½ yard of 40″-wide interfacing

INTERFACING TIP • The heavyweight interfacing will be used on the lining of the bag to help give it structure. If you want your bag to stand up on its own, fusible foam is a good choice. But if you want the bag to have some structure but be soft with some loft, fusible fleece is the way to go. For a little structure but no loft, a heavyweight fusible interfacing, such as Décor-Bond, will give you the desired result.

Cutting

Braid Fabrics

From each of the 5 different plaid fabrics, cut 1 strip 1¼″ × WOF. Using the Mini Braid Template or Template E (page 125), subcut each strip into 10 braid pieces 1¼″ × 3″. If you need a refresher, refer to Cutting the Braid Pieces (page 9).

Braid Accent Fabric

Cut 4 strips ¾″ × WOF. Using the Mini Braid Template or Template A (page 125), subcut a total of 48 braid pieces ¾″ × 3″.

Bag Fabric

Cut 1 strip 12½″ × WOF; subcut into 1 rectangle 12½″ × 18½″, 1 rectangle 7½″ × 14½″, and 1 rectangle 3½″ × 18½″.

Cut 1 strip 6½″ × WOF; subcut into 1 rectangle 6½″ × 8½″, 1 square 6½″ × 6½″, 1 rectangle 6½″ × 4½″, and 1 rectangle 5½″ × 18½″.

Cut 2 strips 2½″ × WOF; subcut into 1 rectangle 2½″ × 18½″, 3 rectangles 2½″ × 8½″, and 1 rectangle 2½″ × 6½″.

Cut 2 strips 5″ × WOF for handles.

Cutting list continued on page 36.

MADE BY
Kate Colleran.

FABRICS ARE FROM
Robert Kaufman Fabrics.

Hummingbirds

Cutting list continued.

Pocket Lining Fabric

Cut 1 strip 8″ × WOF; subcut into 2 rectangles 8″ × 18½″.

Cut 1 strip 10″ × WOF; subcut into 1 rectangle 10″ × 14½″, 1 rectangle 7″ × 6½″, and 1 rectangle 5″ × 6½″.

Lining Fabric

Cut 1 strip 15½″ × WOF; subcut into 2 rectangles 15½″ × 18½″.

Cut 1 strip 7½″ × WOF; subcut into 2 rectangles 7½″ × 18½″.

Lightweight Fusible Interfacing

Cut 1 strip 12½″ × WOF; subcut into 1 rectangle 12½″ × 18½″.

Cut 1 strip 9½″ × WOF; subcut into 1 rectangle 9½″ × 14½″ and 1 rectangle 8½″ × 2½″.

Cut 2 strips 7½″ × WOF; subcut into 2 rectangles 7½″ × 18½″.

Cut 2 strips 6½″ × WOF; subcut into 2 rectangles 6½″ × 8½″, 1 square 6½″ × 6½″, and 1 rectangle 6½″ × 4½″.

Cut 1 strip 5½″ × WOF; subcut into 1 rectangle 5½″ × 18½″.

Cut 4 strips 5″ × WOF for handles.

Cut 1 strip 3½″ × WOF; subcut into 1 rectangle 3½″ × 18½″.

Cut 2 strips 2½″ × WOF; subcut into 1 rectangle 2½″ × 18½″ and 2 rectangles 2½″ × 8½″.

Heavyweight Fusible Interfacing

Cut 1 piece 15½″ × WOF; subcut 2 rectangles 15½″ × 18½″.

ASSEMBLY

Seam allowances are ¼″ unless otherwise noted. Follow the arrows for pressing suggestions.

Making the Short and Long Pieced Braid Units

1. Before you start sewing the braids, you should lay out the fabrics in a pleasing order. Remember, when using strips of different widths, you always want to add pieces the same width in pairs. The pairs don't have to be the same fabric. For my plaids, I picked a pleasing order and then started with one color on the left (light coral plaid) and a different color on the right (green plaid). Each plaid braid pair is followed by a skinny coral braid pair.

PIECING TIP • Don't be intimidated by the skinny braid pieces! They really are no harder to sew than wider pieces; they are just a little trickier to press, as they are small. You really have to watch your seam allowance, as it is the same size as the finished braid piece!

2. Refer to the instructions in Sewing a Basic Braid (page 11). Sew your plaid braid pieces 1¼″ × 3″ and braid accent pieces ¾″ × 3″ together into a long braid, alternating pairs of plaid pieces with pairs of accent pieces. If you need guidance on using strips of various widths, refer to How to Use Varying Size Braid Pieces (page 33).

PIECING TIP • The braid pieces on the left side of the braid will all be even, while on the right side of the braid, the pieces will be jagged. Don't worry! That is how it is supposed to look.

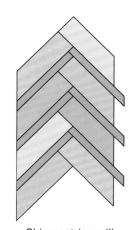

Skinny strips will extend longer on the right side of the braid.

3. Trim the braid into 1 long braid 2½″ × 14½″ and 3 short braids 2½″ × 6½″. If you need guidance on trimming the braid, refer to How to Use Varying Size Braid Pieces (page 33). **A**–**B**

Making the Bag

Making the Bag Pocket Units

1. Sew a short braid unit 2½″ × 6½″ to the top of a bag fabric square 6½″ × 6½″. Press toward the bag fabric. **C**

2. Fuse a lightweight interfacing rectangle 6½″ × 8½″ to the wrong side of the unit from Step 1, following manufacturer's instructions. Set aside.

3. Sew a short braid unit 2½″ × 6½″ to the top of a bag fabric rectangle 2½″ × 6½″. Press toward the bag fabric. The pocket unit should measure 4½″ × 6½″. **D**

4. Fuse a lightweight interfacing rectangle 4½″ × 6½″ to the wrong side of the pocket unit from Step 3, following manufacturer's instructions.

5. Layer the pocket unit right sides together (RST) with the pocket lining fabric rectangle 5″ × 6½″. (Bottom edges will not line up.) Sew the top edges together. **E**

6. Turn the pocket unit right sides out and align the bottom edges. Press the top edge flat. The lining will roll over to the front by ¼″. Topstitch, if desired, in the ditch between the lining and the braid. **F**

POCKET TIP • Cutting the pocket lining piece slightly longer than the pocket unit allows the lining fabric to show from the front. It's just the lining, but it looks like a contrast edging. It's a nice accent when used on all the pockets for the bag.

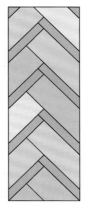

A
Short braid

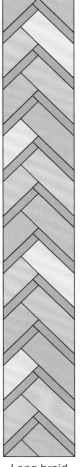

B
Long braid

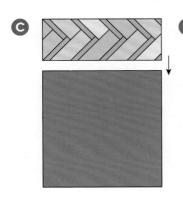

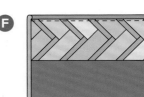

7. Place the pocket unit from Step 6 on top of the unit from Step 2, aligning the bottom edges. Baste the side edges, using an ⅛″ seam, to close the sides of the pocket unit. This unit is the left pocket for the bag front. **G**

8. Fuse a lightweight interfacing rectangle 6½″ × 8½″ to the wrong side of the bag fabric rectangle 6½″ × 8½″, following manufacturer's instructions.

9. Sew a short braid unit 2½″ × 6½″ to the top of a bag fabric rectangle 4½″ × 6½″. Press toward the bag fabric. The pocket unit should measure 6½″ × 6½″. **H**

10. Fuse a lightweight interfacing square 6½″ × 6½″ to the wrong side of the pocket unit, following manufacturer's instructions.

11. Layer the pocket unit RST with the pocket lining fabric rectangle 6½″ × 7″, aligning the top edges. (Bottom edges will not line up.) Sew the top edges. Turn the unit right sides out and align the bottom edges. Press the top edge flat. The lining will roll over to the front by ¼″. Topstitch, if desired, in the ditch between the lining and the braid.

12. Place the pocket unit from Step 11 on top of the unit from Step 8, aligning the bottom edges. Baste the side edges, using an ⅛″ seam, to close the sides of the pocket unit. This unit is the right pocket for the bag front. **I**

Making the Bag Front

1. Fuse corresponding lightweight interfacing pieces to the wrong side of bag fabric pieces, 1 rectangle 5½″ × 18½″, 1 rectangle 2½″ × 18½″, and 3 rectangles 2½″ × 8½″, following manufacturer's instructions.

2. Sew a bag fabric rectangle 2½″ × 8½″ between the left and right pocket units and on both sides. The large pocket unit should measure 8½″ × 18½″. Topstitch, if desired, ⅛″ from the seams on the bag rectangles.

3. Sew the bag fabric rectangle 2½″ × 18½″ to the top and the bag fabric rectangle 5½″ × 18½″ to the bottom of the large pocket unit. The bag front should measure 15½″ × 18½″.

4. Topstitch, if desired, ⅛″ from the top and bottom seams. **J**

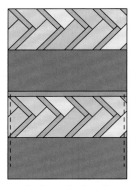

G

Left pocket unit

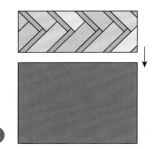

H

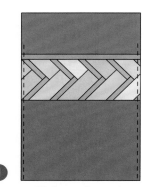

I

Right pocket unit

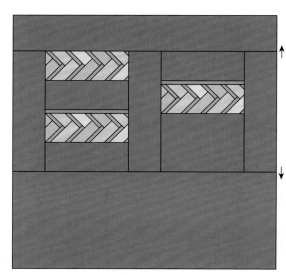

J

Bag front

Making the Bag Back

1. Make a pocket unit by sewing a long braid unit 2½″ × 14½″ to the top of a bag fabric rectangle 7½″ × 14½″. Press toward the rectangle. **K**

2. Fuse a lightweight interfacing rectangle 9½″ × 14½″ to the wrong side of the unit from Step 1, following manufacturer's instructions.

3. Layer the pocket unit RST with the pocket lining fabric 10″ × 14½″ rectangle, aligning the top edges. (Bottom edges will not line up.) Sew the top edges. Align the bottom edges. Press the top edge flat. The lining will roll over to the front by ¼″.

4. Sew the side seams. Turn the pocket unit right sides out and press. Topstitch, if desired, in the ditch between the lining and the braid.

5. Fuse lightweight interfacing to the wrong side of the bag fabric rectangles 12½″ × 18½″ and 3½″ × 18½″, following manufacturer's instructions.

6. Center the pocket unit along the bottom edge on top of the interfaced bag fabric rectangle 12½″ × 18½″. Topstitch the side seams, using a ⅛″ seam.

7. Optional: Topstitch down the center of the pocket unit to create 2 sections. Backstitch at the top edges of the pocket unit.

8. Sew the interfaced bag fabric rectangle 3½″ × 18½″ to the bottom of the bag back. The bag back should measure 15½″ × 18½″. Topstitch, if desired, ⅛″ from the bottom seam. **L**

Putting the Bag Together

1. Cut a 2¼″ square from both lower corners of the bag front and the bag back. **M**

2. Layer the bag front and back together RST and sew the side and bottom seams. Press the seams. Topstitch, if desired, ⅛″ from the side seams and bottom seam.

PRESSING TIP • Press the side seams toward the bag back and the bottom seam in the opposite direction to the bag front so the seams nest together.

3. To make boxed corners, flatten a corner, matching the side seam with the bottom seam. Sew using a ¼″ seam. Backstitch at each end of the seam. Repeat on the other corner of the bag. **N**

K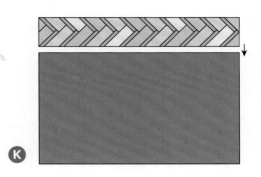

L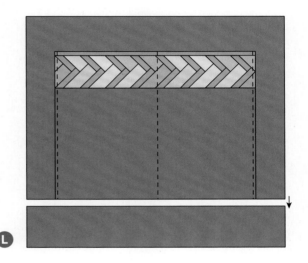

M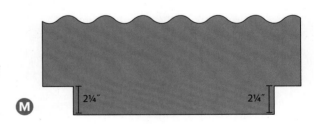
2¼″   2¼″

N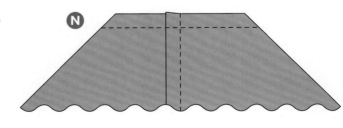

Making the Bag Lining

Making the Lining Pocket Units

1. Fuse a lightweight interfacing to the wrong side of both lining fabric rectangles 7½″ × 18½″, following manufacturer's instructions.

2. Layer the interfaced lining fabric rectangles 7½″ × 18½″ RST with the pocket lining fabric rectangle 8″ × 18½″, aligning the top edges. (Bottom edges will not line up.) Sew the top edges. Press the top edges flat. The lining will roll over to the front by ¼″.

3. Align the bottom edges RST and sew the bottom seam. Turn the pocket unit right side out. Topstitch, if desired, in the ditch between the lining and the pocket. Make 2 pocket units.

4. Fuse a heavyweight interfacing rectangle 15½″ × 18½″ to the wrong side of both lining fabric rectangles 15½″ × 18½″, following manufacturer's instructions.

5. Position a pocket unit on top of a bag lining piece, about 3½″ from the bottom, and baste the side edges using a ⅛″ seam. Topstitch along the bottom edge of the pocket. Repeat on the other lining piece.

6. Optional: On one lining piece, topstitch 2 lines, each about 5¾″ from the sides of the bag, to create 3 pocket sections. On the second piece, topstitch 1 line down the center of the pocket to create 2 sections. Backstitch at the top of the pocket.

Putting the Lining Together

1. Cut a 2¼″ square from both lower corners of both bag lining pieces.

2. Layer the 2 bag lining pieces RST and sew the side seams. Sew the bottom seam, leaving a 6″ opening in the center for turning.

3. To make boxed corners, flatten a corner, matching the side seam with the bottom seam. Sew using a ¼″ seam. Backstitch at each end of the seam. Repeat on the other corner of the lining.

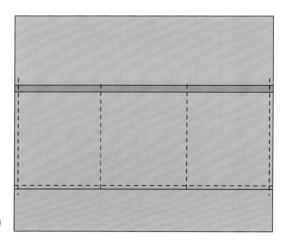

Making the Handles

1. Determine the length you want your handles to be. I cut mine 5″ × 30″ long. The handles will finish 2″ shorter than you cut them. Trim the 5″ × 20″ interfacing strips to the same length as the handle pieces.

2. Fuse the lightweight interfacing to the wrong side of both handle pieces, following the manufacturer's instructions.

3. Fold and press the handle pieces in half lengthwise, wrong sides together. Open the strip, fold the long edges to the center, fold in toward the center, and press again. The handle pieces should measure about 1¼″ wide.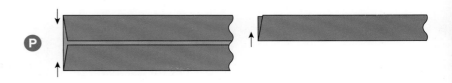

4. Topstitch along the long open edge, about ⅛″ from the edge, and along the other long edge. If desired, topstitch the handle again inside the first seams. I did a total of 5 stitching lines on my handle pieces.

5. Position the handle pieces on the bag 4″ from both side seams, with about ¾″ of the handle extending past the top edge. Be sure not to twist the handle. Baste in place using a ⅛″ seam. Repeat on the other side of the bag with the second handle piece.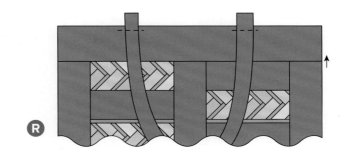

PUTTING THE BAG TOGETHER

1. Tuck the bag inside the lining, RST. Align the side seams. Be sure to tuck the handles down away from the top edge.

2. Sew the top edges of the bag and lining together.

3. Turn the bag right sides out through the opening in the lining. Fold in the raw edges of the opening in the lining and stitch closed. Tuck the lining into the bag and push out the boxed corners.

4. Press the seams along the top edge of the bag and then topstitch about ⅛″ from the edge. Ta-done!

CLEMENTINE

Finished long braid block: 6″ × 42″ • **Finished short braid block:** 6″ × 18″
Finished star block: 12″ × 12″ • **Finished quilt:** 61½″ × 72½″

For this quilt, we are making long braids using strips of four different sizes!

Fabric Selection

This quilt started with a design concept: I wanted the quilt to feel like a formal garden, with the flowers and plants organized in rows. For color, I used my batik line Breezy, as it has a variety of greens. The green braids represent all the plants, leaves, and even the stems of the flowers. The flowers are represented by the pieced block. Granted, the blocks are stars, not flowers, but I chose the oranges and purples to represent a lovely fall flower!

Materials

Yardages are based on 40″-wide fabric.

Light green: ⅜ yard

Medium green: ½ yard

Medium dark green: ⅜ yard

Dark green: ¾ yard

Orange: ⅜ yard

Dark purple: ⅝ yard

Light purple: ⅜ yard

Medium purple: ¼ yard

Orange and purple print: ¼ yard

Background: 3¼ yards

Binding: ⅝ yard

Backing: 4⅝ yards

Batting: 69″ × 80″

Cutting

CUTTING TIP • Pieces marked with an asterisk (*) can be cut oversized for either Half-Square Triangle (HST) or Flying Geese (FG) units.

Light Green

Cut 7 strips 1½″ × WOF. Using the Braid Template or Template L (page 126), subcut 42 braid pieces 1½″ × 6½″. If you need a refresher, refer to Cutting Braid Pieces (page 9).

Medium Green

Cut 7 strips 1¾″ × WOF. Using the Braid Template or Template N (page 127), subcut 42 braid pieces 1¾″ × 6½″.

Medium Dark Green

Cut 7 strips 1¼″ × WOF. Using the Braid Template or Template I (page 125), subcut 42 braid pieces 1¼″ × 6½″.

Dark Green

Cut 21 strips 1″ × WOF. Using the Braid Template or Template D (page 125), subcut 126 braid pieces 1″ × 6½″.

Orange

Cut 3 strips 2⅞″ × WOF*; subcut into 32 squares 2⅞″ × 2⅞″*.

MADE BY
Kate Colleran.

QUILTED BY
Lisa Soderborg of The Quilted Cricket.

FABRICS ARE FROM
the Breezy collection by Kate Colleran for Island Batik.

Dark Purple

Cut 2 strips 5¼″ × WOF*; subcut into 8 squares 5¼″ × 5¼″* and 6 squares 2⅞″ × 2⅞″.

Cut 2 strips 2⅞″ × WOF*; subcut into 26 squares 2⅞″ × 2⅞″*.

Light Purple

Cut 3 strips 2⅞″ × WOF*; subcut into 32 squares 2⅞″ × 2⅞″*.

Medium Purple

Cut 2 strips 2½″ × WOF; subcut into 32 squares 2½″ × 2½″.

Orange and Purple Print

Cut 1 strip 4½″ × WOF; subcut into 8 squares 4½″ × 4½″.

Background

Cut 1 strip 12½″ × WOF; subcut into 2 squares 12½″ × 12½″ and 2 rectangles 12½″ × 6½″.

Cut 2 strips 5¼″ × WOF*; subcut into 8 squares 5¼″ × 5¼″* and 6 squares 2⅞″ × 2⅞″*.

Cut 2 strips 2⅞″ × WOF; subcut into 26 squares 2⅞″ × 2⅞″.

Cut 4 strips 2½″ × WOF; subcut into 4 rectangles 2½″ × 12½″, 32 squares 2½″ × 2½″, and 1 rectangle 2″ × 12½″.

Cut 1 strip 2″ × WOF; subcut into 3 rectangles 2″ × 12½″.

Cut 3 strips 3½″ × WOF; subcut into 4 rectangles 3½″ × 18½″ and 2 rectangles 3½″ × 12½″.

Cut 10 strips 3½″ × WOF; piece ends together and subcut into 4 rectangles 3½″ × 42½″ and 3 sashing strips 3½″ × 68½″.

Cut 7 strips 2½″ × WOF; piece ends together and subcut into 2 side borders 2½″ × 68½″ and 2 top and bottom borders 2½″ × 61½″.

Binding

Cut 8 strips 2¼″ × WOF.

Backing

Cut 2 pieces 80″ × WOF and piece to make a backing about 69″ wide × 80″ long.

ASSEMBLY

Seam allowances are ¼″ unless otherwise noted. Follow the arrows for pressing suggestions.

Making the Braid Block

Before you start sewing the braids, you need to lay out the fabrics in a pleasing order. Remember, when adding strips of different widths, you always want to add pairs of the same width. For example, add two of the light green 1½″-wide braids, one on the left and one on the right, then add two of the dark green skinny 1″-wide braids, then add two of the medium dark green 1¾″-wide braids, then two more dark green skinny 1″-wide braids, and so on. The dark green strips are used in between each pair of the other size strips.

1. Refer to instructions in *Sewing a Basic Braid* (page 11). Sew the various green braid pieces together into a long braid. You will need a braid about 130″ long. If you need guidance on using strips of various widths, refer to How to Use Varying Size Braid Pieces (page 33).

PIECING TIP • The braid pieces on the left side of the braid will all be even, while on the right side of the braid, the pieces will be jagged. Don't worry! That is how it is supposed to look.

2. Trim the braid into 2 long braids 6½″ × 42½″ and 2 short braids 6½″ × 18½″. If you need guidance on trimming the braid, refer to How to Use Varying Size Braid Pieces (page 33). **A** – **B**

CUTTING TIP • When making a really long braid that will be cut into smaller units, I like to cut as I go so I don't have to handle a lengthy braid piece—or in this case, a really, really long braid! Once your braid is long enough, cut off your first long braid segment, then keeping adding pieces to the braid until you can cut the next one, and so on!

Making the Star Block

1. Make 32 FG units from 8 dark purple squares 5¼″ × 5¼″ and 32 orange squares 2⅞″ × 2⅞″. FG units should measure 2½″ × 4½″. If you oversized, trim to size. If you need more information on making FG units, refer to How to Make Flying Geese Units (page 123). **C**

2. Make 32 FG units from 8 background squares 5¼″ × 5¼″ and 32 dark purple squares 2⅞″ × 2⅞″. FG units should measure 2½″ × 4½″. **D**

3. Make 64 HST units from 32 background and 32 light purple squares 2⅞″ × 2⅞″. Press. HST units should measure 2½″ × 2½″. If you oversized the squares, trim to size. If you need more information on making HST units, refer to How to Make Half-Square Triangle Units (page 123). **E**

A

Short braid

B

Long braid

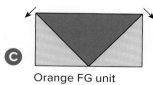

C Orange FG unit

D Dark purple FG unit

E

HST unit

4. Sew a dark purple FG unit to the top of an orange FG unit. Press toward the orange FG unit. The side unit should measure 4½″ × 4½″. Make 4 side units per block for a total of 32 units. **F**

5. Sew 2 HST units, 1 background square 2½″ × 2½″, and 1 medium purple square 2½″ × 2½″ into a Four-Patch unit. Press away from the medium purple square. Make 4 Four-Patch units per block for a total of 32 corner units. **G**

6. Referring to the star block assembly diagram, at right, sew a side unit to both sides of an orange and purple print square 4½″ × 4½″. Press toward the square. The center row should measure 4½″ × 12½″. Make 1 center row per block for a total of 8 rows.

7. Sew a corner unit to both sides of a side unit. Note the rotation of the units. Press toward the corner units. The outer row should measure 4½″ × 12½″. Make 2 outer rows per block for a total of 16 rows.

8. Sew an outer row to the top and bottom of a center row. Swirl the seams; for a refresher, see How to Swirl the Seams (page 124). The Star block should measure 12½″ × 12½″. Make 8 Star blocks. **H**

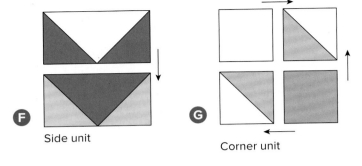

F Side unit

G Corner unit

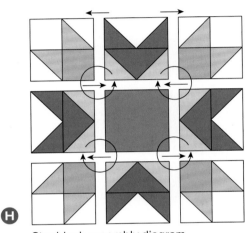

H Star block assembly diagram

MAKING THE QUILT

The quilt is sewn in columns.

1. Sew a background rectangle 3½″ × 42½″ to both sides of a long Braid block. Press toward the background fabric. Make 2 long braid sections.

2. Sew a Star block to the top of a background rectangle 2½″ × 12½″. Press toward the background rectangle.

3. Sew the Star block unit to the top of a long braid unit. Press toward the background rectangle.

4. Sew a background square 12½″ × 12½″ to the bottom of the braid unit. Press toward the background square. Column 1 should measure 12½″ × 68½″. Make 2 of column 1.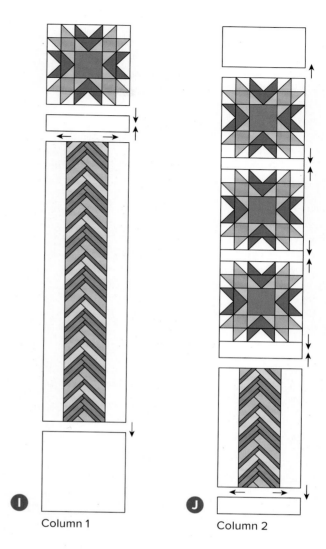

5. Sew 3 Star blocks together in a column, with a background rectangle 2″ × 12½″ between each block. Press toward the background rectangles.

6. Sew a background rectangle 2½″ × 12½″ to the bottom of the Star blocks and a background rectangle 6½″ × 12½″ to the top of the Star blocks. Press toward the background rectangles.

7. Sew a background rectangle 3½″ × 18½″ to both sides of a short braid block. Press toward the background rectangle. Make 2 short braid sections.

8. Sew the braid section to the bottom of the star section. Sew a background rectangle 3½″ × 12½″ to the bottom of the column. Press toward the background rectangles. Column 2 should measure 12½″ × 68½″. Make 2 of column 2.

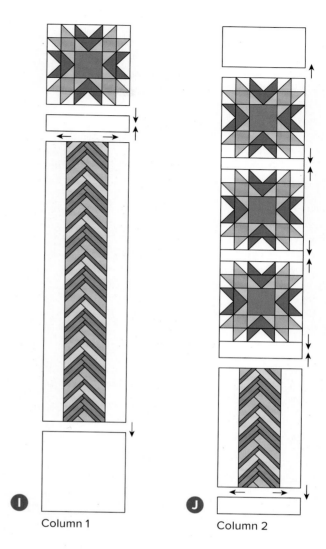

Column 1   Column 2

9. Refer to the quilt assembly diagram below and sew the columns together, with a background sashing strip 3½″ × 68½″ between each column. Press toward the sashing. Note the rotation of the columns. The quilt top should measure 57½″ × 68½″.

10. Sew a background fabric border 2½″ × 68½″ to both sides of the quilt top. Press toward the border.

11. Sew a background fabric border 2½″ × 61½″ to the top and bottom of the quilt top. Press toward the border. The quilt top should measure 61½″ × 72½″. **K**

FINISHING

1. Layer the quilt top with batting and backing and quilt as desired.

2. Bind the quilt.

Quilt assembly diagram

BLUE DAHLIA

Finished short braid block: 5″ × 17½″ • **Finished long braid block:** 5″ × 37½″
Finished quilt: 47½″ × 53½″

For this quilt, we are making long braids using strips of two different sizes to frame this gorgeous panel!

Fabric Selection

The color story of this quilt came from the panel. I used a few of the tone-on-tone fabrics from the flower colors of the panel along with a couple of blues from the line to complement the panel. The idea was to let the panel take center stage and use the braids to add a little interest.

When you're adding a braid around a panel, the size of the braid can be guided by the number of other elements or blocks in the quilt. If the design is simple, the braid can be larger; if there are a lot of other blocks, the braid can be smaller to complement the other design elements.

Materials

Yardages are based on 40″-wide fabric.

Panel: 1 yard

Turquoise: ¾ yard

Braid fabrics: ⅜ yard of 3 fabrics (lavender, aqua, and bright pink) and ¼ yard of 2 fabrics (light pink and yellow). For ease and flexibility, consider purchasing ⅜ yard of all fabrics.

Binding: ½ yard

Backing: 3¼ yards

Batting: 55″ × 61″

Cutting

Panel

Cut panel to 35″ wide × 41″ long.

CUTTING TIP • Most panel quilt patterns include an inner printed border around the panel. It serves to frame the panel but also to work as coping strips, or strips that can be cut bigger or smaller to adjust, or cope, for variations in the size of your panel. The goal is to end up with the quilt center at the size indicated. For this project, the panel is cut to 35″ wide × 41″ long, and the center of the quilt, made up of the panel and the inner borders, should measure 37″ wide × 43″ long. Adjust the inner borders as needed for your panel.

Turquoise

Cut 2 strips 5½″ × WOF; subcut into 2 side outer borders 5½″ × 16″ and 2 top and bottom outer borders 5½″ × 19½″.

Cut 1 strip 1½″ × WOF. Using the Braid Template or Template K (page 126), subcut 4 braid pieces 1½″ × 5¾″. If you need a refresher, refer to Cutting the Braid Pieces (page 9).

Cut 4 strips 1½″ × WOF; piece the ends together diagonally (including the leftover from the previous 1½″ strip) and subcut into 2 side inner borders 1½″ × 41″ and 2 top and bottom inner borders 1½″ × 37″.

Lavender, Aqua, and Bright Pink Braid Fabrics

From each fabric, cut 6 strips 1½″ × WOF. Using the Braid Template or Template K (page 126), subcut 44 braid pieces 1½″ × 5¾″.

Cutting list continued on page 52.

Cutting list continued.

Light Pink and Yellow Braid Fabrics

From each fabric, cut 7 strips 1″ × WOF. Using the Braid Template or Template C (page 125), subcut 44 braid pieces 1″ × 5¾″.

Binding

Cut 6 strips 2¼″ × WOF.

Backing

Cut 2 pieces 55″ × WOF and piece crosswise to make a backing about 55″ wide × 61″ long.

ASSEMBLY

Seam allowances are ¼″ unless otherwise noted. Follow the arrows for pressing suggestions.

Making the Braid Blocks

Before you start sewing the braids, you need to lay out the fabrics in a pleasing order. Remember, when adding strips of different widths, you always want to add pairs of pieces of the same width. They don't have to be the same fabric! For my quilt, the yellow and the light pink strips were cut 1″ wide, and I decided to group them together. Then, I followed with the bright pink and lavender and ended the color set with the aqua braid pieces.

1. Refer to the instructions in Sewing a Basic Braid (page 11). Starting with the **yellow** braid pieces, then using 8 pairs of the yellow, light pink, and bright pink and 7 pairs of the lavender and aqua braid pieces, sew them together into a long braid. If you need guidance on using strips of various widths, refer to How to Use Varying Size Braid Pieces (page 33).

PIECING TIP • The braid pieces on the left side of the braid will all be even, while on the right side of the braid, the pieces will be jagged. Don't worry! That is how it is supposed to look.

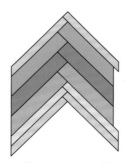

Skinny strips will extend longer on the right side of the braid.

2. Trim the braid to 5½″ × 38″. Repeat to make 2 long braids. If you need guidance on trimming the braid, refer to How to Use Varying Size Braid Pieces (page 33). **Ⓐ**

3. Using 3 pairs of yellow, light pink, and bright pink, and 4 pairs of the lavender and aqua braid pieces, start with the **lavender** braid pieces and sew them together into a short braid.

4. Sew a pair of turquoise braid pieces to the end of the braid.

5. Trim the braid to 5½″ × 18″. Repeat to make 2 short braids. **Ⓑ**

MAKING THE QUILT

1. Refer to the quilt assembly diagram, at right, and sew a turquoise inner border 1½″ × 41″ to the sides of the panel. Press toward the borders.

2. Sew a turquoise inner border 1½″ × 37″ to the top and bottom of the panel. Press toward the borders. The center of the quilt top should measure 37″ wide × 43″ long.

3. Sew a turquoise outer border 5½″ × 19½″ to the top of a short braid. Press toward the turquoise border. The border should measure 5½″ × 37″. Make 2 top and bottom borders.

4. Sew the top and bottom border to the quilt top. Press toward the quilt center.

5. Sew a turquoise outer border 5½″ × 16″ to the bottom of a long braid. Press toward the turquoise border. The border should measure 5½″ × 53½″. Make 2 side borders.

B

Short braid

A

Long braid

C

Quilt assembly diagram

6. Sew the side borders to the sides of the quilt top. Press toward the quilt center. The quilt top should measure 47½˝ wide × 53½˝ long. C

FINISHING

1. Layer the quilt top with batting and backing and quilt as desired.

2. Bind the quilt.

ADDING SQUARES TO YOUR BRAID

This next set of braid quilts adds a square to the mix!

Adding squares is a fun way to add a little dash of color or contrast to your braid. It gives your braid a visual center and acts like a guide, drawing the eye up and down the braid. The math to add squares is easy: Whatever width you cut the strips for your braid pieces, cut the squares the same size. For example, if your braid strips are 2″ wide, cut the square 2″ × 2″.

For my *Arrowleaf* quilt, I made sure to have a full square at the bottom of the braid, but I didn't worry about where the square was cut at the top of the braid.

Detail shot of *Arrowleaf* quilt

For the *Pink Delight* quilt, I wanted the braid to have full squares at the top and the bottom of the braid. To achieve this effect, I added background braid pieces to the braid so the ends of the braids would each have a full square and the white braids would blend into the background of the quilt.

Detail shot of *Pink Delight* quilt

HOW TO ADD SQUARES TO A BASIC BRAID

1. Cut the squares the same width as your braid pieces.

2. Lay out your braid pieces in a pleasing arrangement. Sew the squares to all the left-side braid pieces. Press each seam toward the braid piece except for the first braid; press that one toward the square. **A**

3. Start the braid with a square and sew the first right braid piece to the side of the square. Press toward the square.

4. Sew the first left braid piece with a square to the top of the braid. Press toward the new braid piece. **B**

5. Continue to add braid pieces, next to the right side and then to the left side. **C**

6. Once you have added all the braid pieces, keep the squares centered in the braid and trim the braid to the length and width desired. **D**

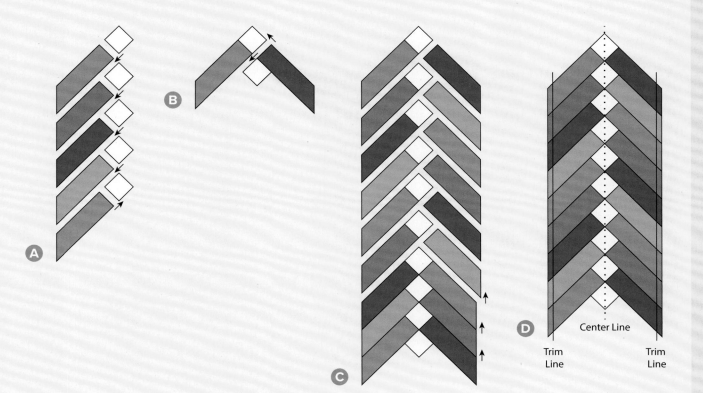

A

B

C

D

Center Line

Trim
Line

Trim
Line

TRIMMING TIP • If you want a full square at the top (pointed end) of the braid block, trim ¼˝ above the top intersection of a full square. If you want a full square at the bottom of the braid, trim ¼˝ below the bottom intersection of a full square.

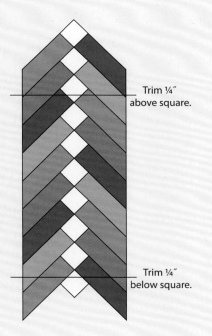

Trim ¼˝
above square.

Trim ¼˝
below square.

ARROWLEAF

Finished braid block: 4″ × 8″ • **Finished center block:** 4″ × 4″
Finished corner block: 8″ × 8″ • **Finished quilt:** 24½″ × 24½″

I love a rainbow! Braids in bold colors create a dramatic design in this mini quilt. The contrast with the off-white background gives it a modern, playful feel.

Fabric Selection

For this quilt, I wanted to use a rainbow of color because, well, rainbow quilts are just so fun! I chose fabrics from the Rainbow Spice line from Moda. For the center squares of the braid, I used a yellow fabric. It provided some contrast with the other colors but didn't overtake the braid—it just added a nice line of color.

Materials

Yardages are based on 40″-wide fabric.

Braid fabrics: ⅛ yard each of 8 different fabrics

Yellow: ¼ yard

Off-white background: ¾ yard

Blue: ¼ yard

Coral: ⅛ yard

Binding: ⅜ yard

Backing: 1 yard

Batting: 32″ × 32″

Cutting

CUTTING TIP • Pieces marked with an asterisk (*) can be cut oversized for either Half-Square Triangles (HST) or Flying Geese (FG) units.

Braid Fabrics

From each of 8 different fabrics, cut 1 strip 1¼″ × WOF. Using the Mini Braid Template or Template F (page 125), subcut 8 braid pieces 1¼″ × 4″ from each fabric. If you need a refresher, refer to Cutting the Braid Pieces (page 9).

Yellow

Cut 1 strip 3¼″ × WOF*; subcut into 2 squares 3¼″ × 3¼″*. Subcut the rest of the strip into 2 long strips: 1 strip 1½″ wide and 1 strip 1¼″ wide. Subcut the 1½″ wide strip into 20 squares 1½″ × 1½″. Subcut the 1¼″ strip into 26 squares 1¼″ × 1¼″.

Cut 1 strip 1¼″ × WOF; subcut into 14 squares 1¼″ × 1¼″.

Cutting list continued on page 58.

MADE BY
Kate Colleran.

QUILTED BY
Lisa Soderborg of The
Quilted Cricket.

FABRICS ARE FROM
*the Rainbow Spice fabric
collection from Sarditty
for Moda Fabrics.*

Cutting list continued.

Off-White Background

Cut 3 strips 2½″ × WOF; subcut into 20 squares 2½″ × 2½″ and 12 rectangles 2½″ × 4½″.

Cut 1 strip 1⅞″ × WOF*; subcut into 10 squares 1⅞″ × 1⅞″* and 8 squares 1½″ × 1½″.

Cut 5 strips 1½″ × WOF; subcut into 4 inner borders 1½″ × 20½″, 12 rectangles 1½″ × 2½″, and 32 squares 1½″ × 1½″.

Cut 2 strips 1¼″ × WOF; using the Mini Braid Template or Template F (page 125), subcut 16 braid pieces 1¼″ × 4″.

Blue

Cut 1 strip 1⅞″ × WOF*; subcut into 2 squares 1⅞″ × 1⅞″* and 4 squares 1½″ × 1½″.

Cut 3 strips 1½″ × WOF; piece the ends together diagonally and subcut into 2 side outer borders 1½″ × 22½″ and 2 top and bottom outer borders 1½″ × 24½″.

Coral

Cut 1 strip 1½″ × WOF; subcut into 8 squares 1½″ × 1½″.

Binding

Cut 3 strips 2¼″ × WOF.

Backing

Cut 1 piece 32″ × 32″.

ASSEMBLY

Seam allowances are ¼″ unless otherwise noted. Follow the pressing arrows shown in the illustrations.

Braid Blocks

1. Organize the fabrics into a pleasing arrangement. For my quilt, I organized the fabrics by color. For the first braid, I started with purple and pink, followed by red and orange, then two greens, ending with two blues. You will make 4 different braids; I chose to start each braid with a different color pair.

2. Each braid needs 2 off-white and 8 colored braid pieces for each side. Once you have the braids laid out in order, sew a yellow 1¼″ square to 2 off-white and 7 of the color left-side braid pieces. Don't add a square to the last left-side color piece. If you need guidance on adding squares to a braid, refer to the How to Add Squares to a Basic Braid (page 54). 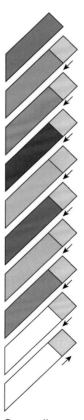 **A**

3. Refer to the instructions in Sewing a Basic Braid (page 11). Using the right braid pieces and the left braid pieces with the squares, and starting with a yellow square and a right-side off-white braid piece, sew the off-white and colored pieces together into a long braid. **B**

A

Sew yellow squares to all but 1 left-side braid piece.

B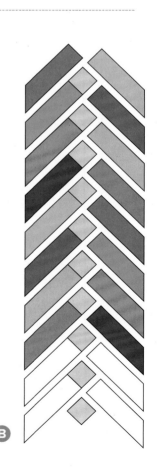

4. Starting at the beginning of the braid, trim the braid straight across ¼″ below the top of the first yellow square. Trim the braid to 4½″ × 8½″. If you need guidance, refer to How to Add Squares to a Basic Braid (page 54). Make a total of 4 braids. **C**

5. Draw a diagonal line corner to corner on the wrong side of 2 off-white squares 1½″ × 1½″. **D**

6. Position 1 square in the upper-left corner of the braid. Sew on the line and trim the seam to ¼″. Press toward the off-white triangle. **E**

7. Position the other off-white square in the upper-right corner of the braid. Sew on the line and trim the seam to ¼″. Press toward the off-white triangle. Repeat on all 4 braids. **F**

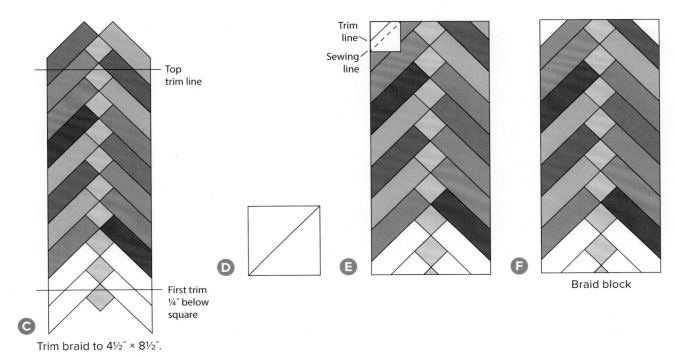

Top trim line

Trim line

Sewing line

First trim ¼″ below square

C

Trim braid to 4½″ × 8½″.

D

E

F

Braid block

Center Block

1. Make 8 FG units from 2 yellow squares 3¼″ × 3¼″ and 8 off-white squares 1⅞″ × 1⅞″. You will only need 6 of the FG units. Flying Geese units should measure 1½″ × 2½″. If you oversized, trim to size. If you need more information on making FG units, refer to How to Make Flying Geese Units (page 123). **G**

2. Sew 1 FG unit to another FG unit. Follow the pressing arrows and press toward one side. Note the rotation of the units. Make 2 pairs.

3. Sew the 2 FG pairs together. Follow the pressing arrows and press toward one side. The center row should measure 2½″ × 4½″. Make 1 row. **H**

G

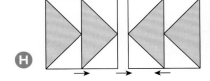

H

4. Sew an off-white square 1½″ × 1½″ to the sides of the remaining 2 FG units. Press toward the off-white squares. The outer rows should measure 1½″ × 4½″. Make 2 outer rows.

5. Sew the rows together. Press toward the outer rows. The center block should measure 4½″ × 4½″. Make 1 center block. **I**

Corner Block

1. Sew 2 off-white and 2 yellow squares 1½″ × 1½″ together into a Four-Patch unit. Swirl the center seam (see How to Swirl the Seams, page 124). Each Four-Patch unit should measure 2½″ × 2½″. Make 8 Four-Patch units. **J**

2. Draw a diagonal line corner to corner on the wrong side of 4 blue squares 1½″ × 1½″. Position a blue square in the upper-left corner of an off-white 2½″ × 4½″ rectangle. Sew on the line and trim the seam to ¼″. Press toward the blue triangle. Make 4. **K**

3. Sew a Four-Patch to the right edge of an off-white square 2½″ × 2½″. Press toward the off-white square.

4. Sew the off-white rectangle with the blue triangle in the corner to the top of the unit from Step 3. Press toward the off-white rectangle. Unit 1 should measure 4½″ × 4½″. Make 4 of unit 1. **L**

5. Sew a coral 1½″ square to the top of a white 1½″ square. Press toward the coral square. Sew an off-white 1½″ × 2½″ rectangle to the left side of the unit. Press toward the off-white rectangle.

6. Sew an off-white square 2½″ × 2½″ to the top of the unit. Press toward the off-white square. Sew an off-white 2½″ × 4½″ rectangle to the right side of the unit. Press toward the off-white rectangle. Unit 2 should measure 4½″ × 4½″. Make a total of 8 of unit 2. **M**

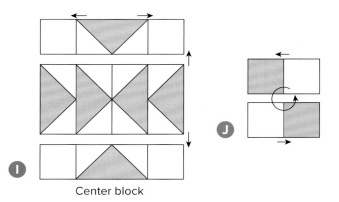

I Center block

J

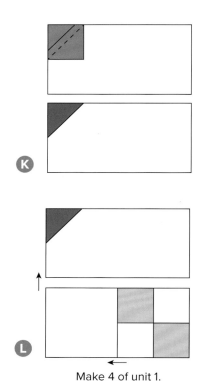

K

L Make 4 of unit 1.

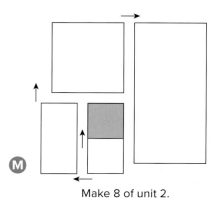

M Make 8 of unit 2.

7. Sew a yellow square 1½″ × 1½″ to the left side of an off-white square 1½″ × 1½″. Press toward the yellow square. Sew a white rectangle 1½″ × 2½″ to the bottom of the unit. Press toward the off-white rectangle.

8. Sew a white square 2½″ × 2½″ to the right side of a Four-Patch unit. Press toward the off-white square.

9. Sew a white square 2½″ × 2½″ to the left side of the unit from Step 7. Press toward the off-white square. Sew the 2 units into a Four-Patch unit. Swirl the center seam. Unit 3 should measure 4½″ × 4½″. Make 4 of unit 3. **N**

10. Sew a unit 1 to the left side of a unit 2 and press toward unit 2. Sew a unit 3 to the right side of a unit 2 and press toward unit 2. Sew the 2 units you just made into a Four-Patch. Note the rotation of the units. Swirl the center seam. The corner block should measure 8½″ × 8½″. Make 4 corner blocks. **O**

11. Make 4 HST units from 2 white and 2 blue squares 1⅞″ × 1⅞″. Press toward the blue squares. HST units should measure 1½″ × 1½″. If you oversized the squares, trim to size. If you need more information on making HST units, refer to How to Make Half-Square Triangle Units (page 123). **P**

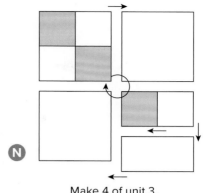

Make 4 of unit 3.

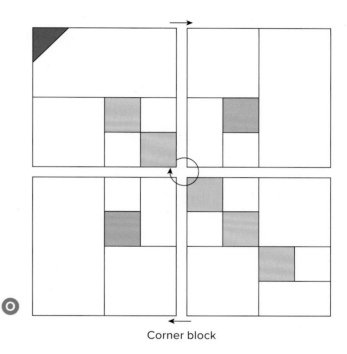

Corner block

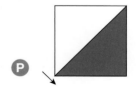

MAKING THE QUILT

1. Refer to the quilt assembly diagram below and sew a braid block to both sides of a center block. Note the direction of the braid blocks. Press toward the center block. The center row should measure 4½˝ × 20½˝. Make 1 center row.

2. Sew a corner block to both sides of a braid block. Note the direction of both blocks. Press toward the corner blocks. The outer row should measure 8½˝ × 20½˝. Make 2 outer rows.

3. Sew the rows together. Swirl the center seams. The quilt top should measure 20½˝ × 20½˝.

4. Sew an off-white inner border 1½˝ × 20½˝ to the sides of the quilt top. Press toward the border.

5. Sew 1 HST unit to both ends of the top and bottom inner borders 1½˝ × 20½˝. Press toward the border. Note the rotation of the HST unit. Sew the border to the top and bottom of the quilt top. Press toward the border.

6. Sew a blue outer border 1½˝ × 22½˝ to the sides of the quilt top. Press toward the blue border. Sew a blue outer border 1½˝ × 24½˝ to the top and the bottom of the quilt top. Press toward the blue border. The quilt top should measure 24½˝ × 24½˝.

Quilt assembly

FINISHING

1. Layer the quilt top with batting and backing and quilt as desired.

2. Bind the quilt.

PINK DELIGHT

Finished braid block: 7″ × 44″ • **Finished quilt:** 37½″ × 48½″

Pink and white is a classic color scheme for a crib quilt. Adding various shades from orange-red to bright pink to soft violet along with the deep blue squares helps the quilt feel a little more modern!

Fabric Selection

I chose fabrics that had a tone-on-tone look to them. I used a variety of pink, red, orange, and violet fabrics so the braids had lots of color and movement. The deep blue squares provide a nice contrast along with a sense of grounding the braids. The crisp white background helps the quilt feel fresh!

Materials

Yardages are based on 40″-wide fabric.

Braid fabrics: ¼ yard each of 8 different fabrics

Deep blue: ⅜ yard

White background: 1⅜ yards

Binding: ½ yard

Backing: 2⅝ yards

Batting: 45″ × 56″

Cutting

Braid Fabrics

From each of 8 different fabrics, cut 2 strips 1¾″ × WOF. Using the Braid Template or Template M (page 126), subcut 12 braid pieces 1¾″ × 6¼″ from each fabric. If you need a refresher, refer to Cutting the Braid Pieces (page 9).

From 1 of the braid fabrics, cut 1 strip 1¾″ × WOF; subcut into 6 rectangles 1¾″ × 3″.

From 1 of the braid fabrics, cut 1 strip 1¾″ × WOF; subcut into 6 rectangles 1¾″ × 4¼″.

CUTTING TIP • If you want your center units to be scrappy, cut the 1¾″ × 3″ and the 1¾″ × 4¼″ rectangles from a variety of braid fabrics.

Deep Blue

Cut 1 strip 3″ × WOF; subcut into 3 squares 3″ × 3″.

Cut 3 strips 1¾″ × WOF; subcut into 61 squares 1¾″ × 1¾″.

Cutting list continued on page 66.

MADE BY
Kate Colleran.

QUILTED BY
Lisa Soderborg of The
Quilted Cricket.

FABRICS ARE FROM
*the Spotsy fabric
collection from
QT Fabrics.*

Cutting list continued.

White Background

Cut 1 strip 45″ × WOF. From the 45″ length of fabric (LOF), subcut 4 sashing strips 4½″ × 44½″ and 2 top and bottom border strips 2½″ × 37½″.

Cut 9 strips 1¾″ × LOF. Using the Braid Template or Template M (page 126), subcut 2 strips into 16 braid pieces 1¾″ × 6¼″.

Unfold 3 of the 1¾″ × LOF strips into a single layer and with the **right** side of the fabric up, and using the Braid Template or Template M (page 126), subcut 25 right braid pieces 1¾″ × 6¼″.

Unfold 4 of the 1¾″ × LOF strips into a single layer and with the **wrong** side of the fabric facing up, and using the Braid Template or Template O (page 127), subcut 25 left braid pieces 1¾″ × 7½″.

Binding

Cut 5 strips 2¼″ × WOF.

Backing

Cut 2 pieces 45″ × WOF. Piece together crosswise to make a backing about 45″ wide × 56″ long.

ASSEMBLY

Seam allowances are ¼″ unless otherwise noted. Follow the arrows for pressing suggestions.

Braid Blocks

There are three different braids. Each braid starts with the same center unit, and then we add braid pieces to the top and bottom. The difference is how many white and colored braid pieces we add to each!

Organize the braid fabrics into a pleasing arrangement. For my quilt, with my assortment of pinks, purples, and reds, I grouped the pieces by color and kept similar colors or values separated.

Making the Braid Center Unit

1. Sew a braid fabric 1¾″ × 3″ rectangle to both sides of the deep blue square 3″ × 3″. Press toward the square.

2. Sew a deep blue square 1¾″ × 1¾″ to the end of the braid fabric 1¾″ × 4¼″ rectangle. Press toward

the square. The unit should measure 1¾″ × 5½″. Make 2 units.

3. Sew a unit from Step 2 to the top and bottom of the center unit. The center unit should measure 5½″ × 5½″. Make 3 center units. **A**

Making Braid 1

1. Select 3 colored and 1 white left braid pieces 1¾″ × 6¼″ and 3 white left braid pieces 1¾″ × 7½″. Select 3 colored and 4 white right braid pieces 1¾″ × 6¼″.

2. Sew a deep blue square 1¾″ × 1¾″ to the 3 colored and 1 white left braid pieces 1¾″ × 6¼″. Press toward the braid piece. If you need guidance on adding squares to a braid, refer to Adding Squares to Your Braid (page 54). **B**

3. Turn a center unit so it is on point. Refer to the instructions in Sewing a Basic Braid (page 11). Starting at the top, sew the first right-side colored braid piece to the right side of the center unit. Press toward the braid piece.

4. Sew the first left-side colored braid unit, with a deep blue square, to the top of the braid. Press toward the braid piece. **C**

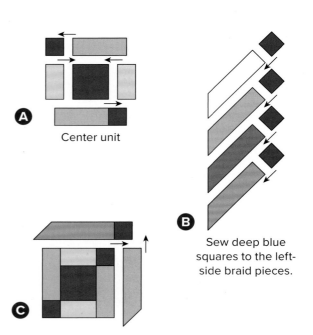

A Center unit

B Sew deep blue squares to the left-side braid pieces.

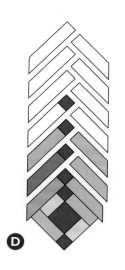

D

E

F

– First trim ¼″ above deep blue square.

G

Trim braid 1 to 7½″ × 44½″.

5. Continue to add the pieces to the right and then the left of the braid. **D**

6. Rotate the braid. **E**

7. Select 15 colored and 1 white left braid pieces 1¾″ × 6¼″ and 4 white left braid pieces 1¾″ × 7½″. Select 15 colored and 5 white right braid pieces 1¾″ × 6¼″.

8. Sew a deep blue square 1¾″ × 1¾″ to the 15 colored and 1 white left braid pieces 1¾″ × 6¼″. Press toward the braid piece.

9. Starting on the right side of the center unit, add the braid pieces to the braid. **F**

10. Rotate the braid so the center unit is closer to the top of the braid. Trim across the top of the braid ¼″ above the top intersection with the top deep blue square.

11. Keeping the deep blue squares centered in the braid, trim the braid to 7½″ × 44½″. If you need guidance, refer to Adding Squares to Your Braid (page 54). **G**

Making Braid 2

Braid 2 is built in the same manner as braid 1: adding squares to the left-side braid pieces and building the braid from the center unit in two directions. It just uses a different mix of braid pieces.

1. Select 8 colored and 2 white left braid pieces 1¾″ × 6¼″ and 5 white left braid pieces 1¾″ × 7½″. Select 8 colored and 7 white right braid pieces 1¾″ × 6¼″.

2. Sew a deep blue square 1¾″ × 1¾″ to the 8 colored and 2 white left braid pieces 1¾″ × 6¼″. Press toward the braid piece.

3. Refer to Steps 3–5 of braid 1 and add the braid pieces to the center unit.

4. Rotate the braid. Select 4 colored and 2 white left braid pieces 1¾″ × 6¼″ and 5 white left braid pieces 1¾″ × 7½″. Select 4 colored and 7 white right braid pieces 1¾″ × 6¼″.

5. Sew a deep blue square 1¾″ × 1¾″ to the 4 colored and 2 white left braid pieces 1¾″ × 6¼″. Press toward the braid piece.

6. Starting on the right side of the center unit, add the braid pieces to the braid.

7. Rotate the braid so the center unit is closer to the bottom of the braid. Trim across the bottom of the braid 5″ from the bottom point of the last deep blue square.

8. Keeping the deep blue squares centered in the braid, trim the braid to 7½″ × 44½″. **H**

Making Braid 3

Braid 3 is built in the same manner as the first two braids!

1. Select 6 colored and 1 white left braid pieces 1¾″ × 6¼″ and 5 white left braid pieces 1¾″ × 7½″. Select 6 colored and 6 white right braid pieces 1¾″ × 6¼″.

2. Sew a deep blue square 1¾″ × 1¾″ to the 6 colored and 1 white left braid pieces 1¾″ × 6¼″. Press toward the braid piece.

3. Refer to Steps 3–5 of braid 1 and add the braid pieces to the center unit.

4. Rotate the braid. Select 11 colored and 1 white left braid pieces 1¾″ × 6¼″ and 3 white left braid pieces 1¾″ × 7½″. Select 11 colored and 4 white right braid pieces 1¾″ × 6¼″.

5. Sew a deep blue square 1¾″ × 1¾″ to the 11 colored and 1 white left braid pieces 1¾″ × 6¼″. Press toward the braid piece.

6. Starting on the right side of the center unit, add the braid pieces to the braid.

7. Rotate the braid so the center unit is closer to the top of the braid. Trim across the **bottom** of the braid ¼″ below the lower intersection with the bottom deep blue square.

8. Keeping the deep blue squares centered in the braid, trim the braid to 7½″ × 44½″. **I**

H

First trim 5″ below bottom deep blue square.

Trim braid 2 to 7½″ × 44½″.

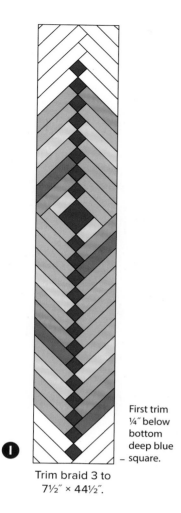

First trim ¼″ below bottom deep blue square.

Trim braid 3 to 7½″ × 44½″.

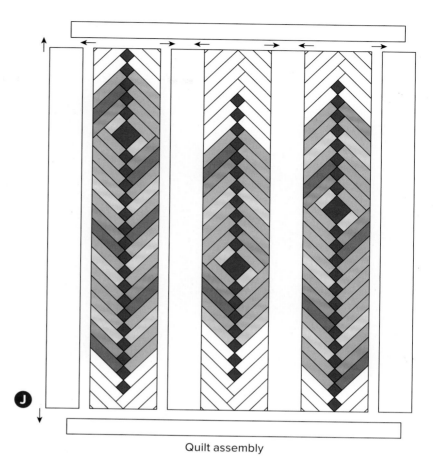

Quilt assembly

MAKING THE QUILT

1. Sew 2 white sashing strips 4½″ × 44½″ between the braids. Press toward the sashing strip.

2. Sew a white sashing strip 4½″ × 44½″ to the sides of the quilt top. Press toward the sashing.

3. Sew a white border strip 2½″ × 37½″ to the top and bottom of the quilt top. Press toward the border. **J**

FINISHING

1. Layer the quilt top with batting and backing and quilt as desired.

2. Bind the quilt.

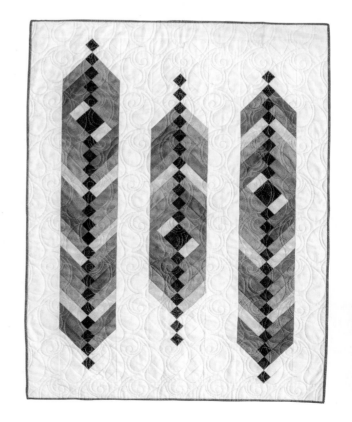

DAISY CHAIN

Finished block: 12″ × 12″ • **Finished quilt:** 78½″ × 90½″

For this quilt, we are making our block look like a braid, but we aren't actually making a braid. So, I guess this quilt is a faux braid!

Fabric Selection

I wanted to use a rainbow of solid colors, and I chose the Kona solid line from Robert Kaufman because it has such a great range of colors. It was hard to narrow down my choices to just seven different colors. My rainbow is not in pure primary colors; I went for slightly softer tints.

When picking your fabrics, you can absolutely use prints, but I would suggest keeping a good value change between the colored fabrics and the pieces where I used black and white. You don't need to use the same colors—just make sure you have high-value contrast so the design stands out!

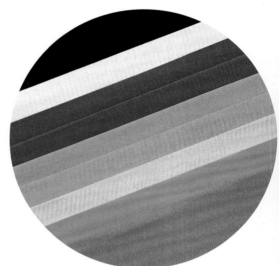

Materials

Yardages are based on 40″-wide fabric.

Colored fabrics: ⅝ yard each of 7 different fabrics

Black contrast: 2⅜ yards

White background: 4 yards

Binding: ¾ yard

Backing: 7¼ yards

Batting: 86″ × 98″

Cutting

Colored Fabrics

From each of 7 different fabrics, cut 7 strips 2½″ × WOF. Subcut 6 strips into 12 rectangles 2½″ × 10½″ and 12 rectangles 2½″ × 6½″. Set aside 1 strip of each fabric for strip sets.

Black Contrast

Cut 23 strips 2½″ × WOF; subcut 16 strips into 252 squares 2½″ × 2½″. Set aside 7 strips for strip sets.

Cut 9 strips 2½″ × WOF; piece the ends together and subcut 2 side outer borders 2½″ × 86½″ and 2 top and bottom outer borders 2½″ × 78½″.

White Background

Cut 11 strips 4½″ × WOF; subcut into 84 squares 4½″ × 4½″.

Cut 29 strips 2½″ × WOF; subcut into 84 rectangles 2½″ × 8½″ and 84 rectangles 2½″ × 4½″.

Cut 9 strips 1½″ × WOF; piece the ends together and subcut 2 side inner borders 1½″ × 84½″ and 2 top and bottom inner borders 1½″ × 74½″.

Binding

Cut 9 strips 2¼″ × WOF.

Backing

Cut 3 pieces 86″ × WOF and piece crosswise to make a backing about 86″ wide × 98″ long.

MADE BY
Kate Colleran.

QUILTED BY
Lisa Soderborg of The
Quilted Cricket.

FABRICS ARE FROM
*the Kona solids collection
from Robert Kaufman.*

71

ASSEMBLY

Seam allowances are ¼˝ unless otherwise noted. Follow the arrows for pressing suggestions.

You will be making 7 different blocks, but they all have the same construction; they just have a different colored fabric. Make 6 blocks of each color.

Braid Block

1. Sew a black 2½˝ × WOF strip to a colored 2½˝ × WOF strip. Press toward the black strip.

2. Subcut strip set into 12 units 2½˝ × 4½˝.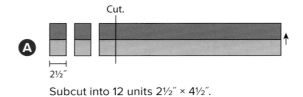

3. Sew 2 units together to make a Four-Patch. Swirl the center seam and press flat. For a refresher, see How to Swirl the Seams (page 124). Make 6 Four-Patch units. **B**

4. Sew a white 2½˝ × 4½˝ rectangle to the right edge of the Four-Patch unit. Press toward the Four-Patch unit.

5. Sew a black square 2½˝ × 2½˝ to a white rectangle 2½˝ × 4½˝. Press toward the black square.

6. Sew the unit from Step 5 to the top of the Four-Patch unit. Swirl the center seam and press flat. **C**

Cut.

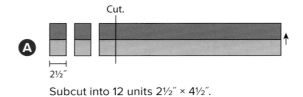

Subcut into 12 units 2½˝ × 4½˝.

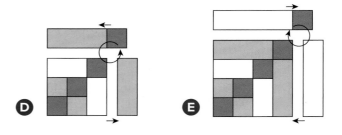

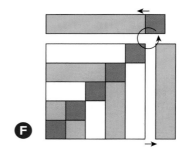

7. Sew a colored 2½˝ × 6½˝ rectangle to the right edge of the block. Press toward the colored rectangle.

8. Sew a black square 2½˝ × 2½˝ to a colored 2½˝ × 6½˝ rectangle. Press toward the colored rectangle.

9. Sew the unit from Step 8 to the top of the block. Swirl the center seam and press flat. **D**

10. Sew a white rectangle 2½˝ × 8½˝ to the right edge of the block. Press toward the block.

11. Sew a black square 2½˝ × 2½˝ to a white rectangle 2½˝ × 8½˝. Press toward the black square.

12. Sew the unit from Step 11 to the top of the block. Swirl the center seam and press flat. **E**

13. Sew a colored rectangle 2½˝ × 10½˝ to the right edge of the block. Press toward the colored rectangle.

14. Sew a black square 2½˝ × 2½˝ to a colored rectangle 2½˝ × 10½˝. Press toward the colored rectangle.

15. Sew the unit from Step 14 to the top of the block. Swirl the center seam and press flat. The block should measure 12½˝ × 12½˝. Repeat to make 6 blocks. **F**

16. Draw a diagonal line corner to corner on the wrong side of 12 white squares 4½″ × 4½″.

17. Position a white square in the upper-left corner of the block. Sew on the line and trim the seam to ¼″. Press toward the white triangle. **G**–**I**

18. Draw a diagonal line corner to corner on the wrong side of 12 black squares 2½″ × 2½″.

19. Position a black square in the upper-left corner of the block on top of the white triangle. Sew on the line and trim the seam to ¼″. Press toward the black triangle. **J**–**K**

20. Repeat Steps 16–19 in the lower-right corner. The block should measure 12½″ × 12½″. Make 6 blocks of each of the 7 colored fabrics. For a total of 42 blocks. **L**

MAKING THE QUILT

You can set the blocks in many different arrangements. I set the quilt with each color in diagonal rows, but you could put the colors in a line or mix them up!

1. Refer to the quilt assembly diagram (page 74) and place the blocks as indicated. The quilt has 7 rows with 6 blocks in each row. Sew the blocks into rows. Press each row in one direction; alternate the pressing direction of the rows. Note the rotation of the blocks in each row.

2. Sew the rows together. The quilt top should measure 72½″ wide × 84½″ long.

3. Sew the white side inner border 1½″ × 84½″ to the sides of the quilt top. Press toward the border.

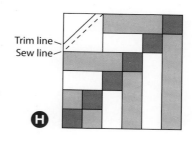

Trim line
Sew line

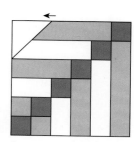

Sew on the line, trim, and press toward the white triangle.

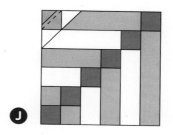

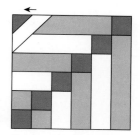

Sew on the line, trim, and press toward the black triangle.

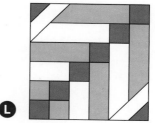

Repeat in the lower-right corner.

4. Sew the white top and bottom inner border 1½″ × 74½″ to the quilt top. Press toward the border.

5. Sew the black side outer border 2½″ × 86½″ to the sides of the quilt top. Press toward the black border.

6. Sew the black top and bottom outer border 2½″ × 78½″ to the quilt top. Press toward the black border. The quilt top should measure 78½″ wide × 90½″ long.

FINISHING

1. Layer the quilt top with batting and backing and quilt as desired.

2. Bind the quilt.

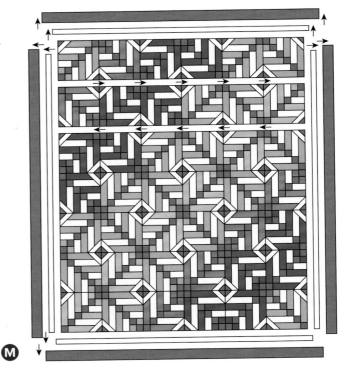

Quilt assembly

Quilt with blocks set in rows of color

USING PIECED STRIPS IN YOUR BRAID

Another way to add interest and variety in your braid is to create pieced strips.

There are different ways to create pieced strips. One way is to sew long strips of fabric together and then subcut the strip sets into braid pieces, as I did with the *Delphinium* pillows.

When you create a strip set and then cut the braid pieces, you get two different-looking braids. For the pillows, I used one braid in one pillow and the other one in the second pillow.

For the pillows, I cut both of my strips the same width, but you could make them different sizes.

Detail shot of braid from one pillow

Detail shot of the braid from the second pillow

Another way to create pieced strips is to sew squares and rectangles together, as I did with the *Zinnia* runner. I sewed pieces together and then sewed the pieced units into braids. For the runner, I didn't cut the pieced units into angled braid pieces.

Why? One reason to use the angled edge is to know where to trim the sides of the braid. But in the runner, the cuts to the side of the braid were made by using a center point for reference, so cutting the pieced rectangles into braids was not necessary!

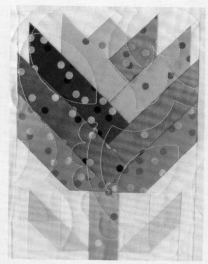

Detail shot of the flower braid

Detail shot of braid in *Zinnia* runner

There are many ways to use pieced units to create new looks in a braid. Let's try these next braid projects and get a feel for some different techniques!

For the *Pink Impressions* quilt, I used squares and rectangles, but I used the stitch and flip technique to create angles within the braid pieces. And just like that, the braid became a flower!

ZINNIA

Finished center braid block: 8½″ × 26″
Finished side braid blocks: 8½″ × 8½″ • **Finished runner:** 13″ × 47½″

Table runners are so much fun to make, to decorate with, or to give as a gift!

Fabric Selection

I wanted a bright table runner that would perk up my table when the weather was drab. I selected the braid fabrics in pairs, a light and a dark each of blue, pink, orange, and yellow-green. The dark blue print in the center grounds the runner and pulls all the colors together.

Materials

Yardage is based on 40″-wide fabric.

Braid fabrics: ⅛ yard each of 4 different light colored fabrics, ⅛ yard of 3 different dark colored fabrics, ¼ yard of 1 dark fabric (dark blue)

White background and border fabric: ⅝ yard

Dark blue multiprint: ¼ yard

Binding: ⅜ yard

Backing: 1⅝ yards

Batting: 22″ × 55″

BATTING TIP • A good batting to use in a table runner is thin or low loft. Warm and White from The Warm Company is a good option, as is fusible fleece.

Cutting

Braid Fabrics

From the dark blue fabric, cut 2 strips 2″ × WOF. Subcut into 2 rectangles 2″ × 9½″ and 6 rectangles 2″ × 4½″.

From the light blue fabric, cut 1 strip 2″ × WOF. Subcut into 2 rectangles 2″ × 6½″ and 6 rectangles 2″ × 3″.

From each of the 3 other light fabrics, cut 1 strip 2″ × WOF. Subcut into 4 rectangles 2″ × 3″.

From each of the 3 other dark fabrics, cut 1 strip 2″ × WOF. Subcut into 4 rectangles 2″ × 4½″.

White Background and Border Fabric

Cut 6 strips 2″ × WOF; subcut into 8 rectangles 2″ × 7″, 10 rectangles 2″ × 5″, 32 rectangles 2″ × 4½″, and 2 rectangles 2″ × 3½″.

Cut 3 strips 2½″ × WOF; piece the ends together and subcut into 2 outer borders 2½″ × 43½″ and 2 outer borders 2½″ × 13″.

CUTTING TIP • You may prefer to wait to cut the borders until after you piece the braid blocks together. Then, measure the length of your pieced runner and cut the borders to the size needed.

Cutting list continued on page 78.

Cutting list continued.

Dark Blue Multiprint Fabric

Cut 1 strip 3½″ × WOF; subcut into 1 square 3½″ × 3½″ and 2 squares 2″ × 2″.

Binding

Cut 4 strips 2¼″ × WOF.

Backing

Cut 1 piece 22″ wide × 55″ long.

ASSEMBLY

Seam allowances are ¼″ unless otherwise noted. Follow the arrows for pressing suggestions.

Making the Pieced Braid Units

For these braids, we won't be cutting the angled edge. Because we will be using the center square and top points of the braid to trim, we already have our guide!

1. Sew 4 white rectangles 2″ × 4½″ to 4 light pink, orange, yellow-green, and blue rectangles 2″ × 3″. Press toward the light fabrics. Light pieced braid units should measure 2″ × 7″. You will have 2 light blue 2″ × 3″ rectangles left over. **A**

2. Sew 4 white rectangles 2″ × 4½″ to 4 dark pink, orange, yellow-green, and blue rectangles 2″ × 4½″. Press toward the dark fabrics. Dark pieced braid units should measure 2″ × 8½″. You will have 2 dark blue rectangles 2″ × 4½″ left over. **B**

Making the Center Braid Block

1. Refer to the center unit assembly diagram (next page) and sew a white rectangle 2″ × 3½″ to opposite sides of the dark blue multiprint square 3½″ × 3½″. Press toward the square.

2. Sew a dark blue multiprint 2″ × 2″ to a white rectangle 2″ × 5″. Press toward the square. Make 2 units.

3. Sew the units from Step 2 to the top and bottom of the center square unit. Press toward the center square.

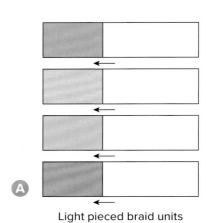

Light pieced braid units

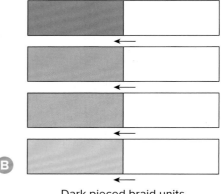

Dark pieced braid units

4. Sew a light blue rectangle 2″ × 6½″ to opposite sides of the center square. *Note the rotation of the small dark blue squares.* Press toward the rectangles.

5. Sew a dark blue rectangle 2″ × 9½″ to the top and bottom of the center square. Press toward the rectangles. The center unit should measure 9½″ × 9½″.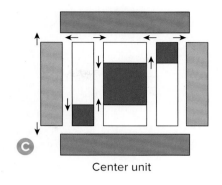

6. Rotate the center unit so the block is on point and a dark blue rectangle is on the upper-left side. Starting on the right side, sew a light pink pieced braid unit 2″ × 7″ to the right side of the center unit. Press toward the pieced braid unit. *Note: The braid unit will not extend to the end of the center unit.*

7. Sew a dark pink pieced braid unit 2″ × 8½″ to the left side of the center unit. Press toward the pieced braid unit. *Note: The braid unit will not extend to the end of the center unit.*

8. Repeat Steps 6–7 with the orange pieced braid units, followed by the yellow-green pieced braid units, and end with the blue pieced braid units.

9. Line up the white rectangle 2″ × 7″ with the lower edge of the last braid unit on the right side of the block and sew to the side of the block. The white rectangle will not go to the top of the block.

10. Sew a white rectangle 2″ × 7″ to the left side of the block, lining it up with the lower edge of the last braid piece.

11. Repeat Steps 9–10 to add a white rectangle 2″ × 5″ to both sides of the block. Yes, it looks a little crazy!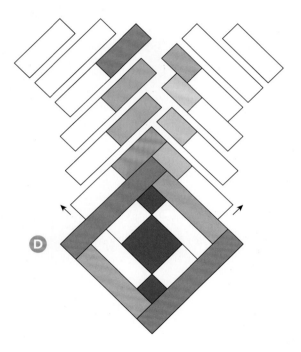

12. Turn the block around and repeat Steps 6–11 on the other side of the block.

13. Trim the ends of the block ½″ past the top point of the yellow-green braid on both ends. The block should be 26½″ long.

Center unit

14. Keeping the block centered on the small blue squares and the points of the braid, trim the center braid block to 9″ wide. **E** – **F**

CUTTING TIP • If your runner is not 26½″ long after you trim to ½″ past the top point of the yellow-green braid, don't worry! When we are sewing so many seams, it can be a little off. When you are done sewing the three braid blocks together, measure the length of your runner and make adjustments to the borders as needed.

Making the Braid Side Blocks

1. Sew a dark blue rectangle 2″ × 4½″ to the top of a light blue rectangle 2″ × 3″. The light blue rectangle is on the right side. Press toward the dark blue rectangle.

2. Starting on the right side, sew a light pink pieced braid unit 2″ × 7″ to the braid. Press toward the light pink unit.

3. Sew a dark pink pieced braid unit 2″ × 8½″ to the left side of the braid. Press toward the dark pink unit.

4. Repeat Steps 2–3 with the orange units, then the yellow-green units, and end with a set of the blue units.

5. Line up the white rectangle 2″ × 7″ with the lower edge of the last braid unit on the right side of the block and sew to the side of the block. The white rectangle will not go to the top of the block.

6. Sew a white rectangle 2″ × 7″ to the left side of the block, lining up with the lower edge of the last braid piece.

7. Repeat Steps 5–6 to add a white rectangle 2″ × 5″ to both sides of the block.

8. Trim the ends of the block ½″ past the top point of the yellow-green braid at the top of the braid. Trim the other end of the braid so the block is 9″ long.

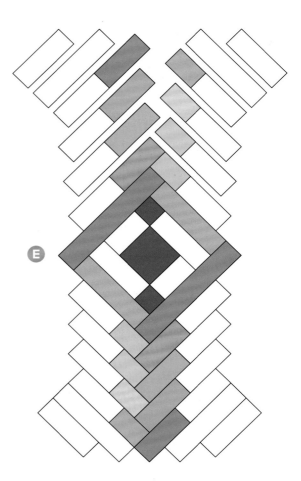

E

F

Trim ½″ above intersection.

Trim ½″ below intersection.

Center braid block

9. Keeping the block centered on the points of the braid, trim the side braid block to 9″ wide. Make 2 side blocks. **G** – **H**

Making the Runner

1. Refer to the runner assembly diagram below and sew a braid side block to both ends of the braid center block. Note the rotation of the braid side blocks; the top of the side blocks should be next to the center block. Press toward one side.

2. Sew a white border 2½″ × 43½″ to both long sides of the runner. Press toward the border.

3. Sew a white border 2½″ × 13″ to the short ends of the runner. Press toward the border. The runner should measure 13″ wide × 47½″ long. **I**

FINISHING

1. Layer the runner top with batting and backing and quilt as desired.

2. Bind the runner.

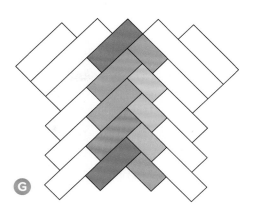

G

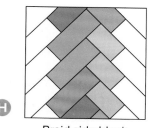

Trim ½″ above intersection.

H

Braid side block

I

Runner assembly diagram

DELPHINIUM

Finished braid block: 3″ × 11½″ • **Finished pillow:** 14½″ × 14½″

Pillows are such a fun way to liven up your decorating quickly and easily. Choose a color scheme to match your decor or one that has a seasonal flavor!

Fabric Selection

I raided my stash and found a few fat eighths from a fabric line called Lagoon by Cotton and Steel. I added a variety of white fabrics and then searched for a binding fabric that would add a little pop of color to the pillows. Although the unexpected color of the binding is not in any of the fabrics on the front of the pillows, I did pull it from one on the back of the pillow!

Materials

Yardage is based on 40″-wide fabric. Fabric requirements shown make 2 pillows.

Braid fabrics: ⅛ yard each of 5 different colored fabrics and ⅛ yard each of 5 different white fabrics

White sashing and border fabric: ⅜ yard

Back: ¾ yard

Binding: ⅜ yard

Lightweight fusible interfacing: 1¼ yards of 20″ wide interfacing

Batting or fusible fleece: 2 pieces 18″ × 18″

2 pillow forms 14″ × 14″

2 nylon zippers 16″ or longer

BATTING TIP • If you plan to quilt the front of your pillow, which I prefer to do, batting or fleece works well. If you want to add a little loft to the front of the pillow but don't want to quilt it, fusible fleece keeps things from shifting around.

Cutting

Braid Fabrics

From each of the 5 different colored fabrics, cut 2 strips 1″ × WOF.

From each of the 5 different white fabrics, cut 3 strips 1″ × WOF.

White Sashing and Border Fabric

Cut 4 strips 1¾″ × WOF; subcut into 4 rectangles 1¾″ × 14½″ and 8 rectangles 1¾″ × 12″.

Back

Cut 2 strips 9½″ × WOF; subcut into 4 rectangles 9½″ × 14½″.

Binding

Cut 4 strips 2¼″ × WOF.

Lightweight Fusible Interfacing

Cut 4 rectangles 9½″ × 14½″.

ASSEMBLY

Seam allowances are ¼″ unless otherwise noted. Follow the arrows for pressing suggestions.

Making the Braid Blocks

1. Organize the fabrics into sets of 1 white and 1 colored fabric strips 1″. Sew the colored fabric strip to the top of the white strip. Press toward the colored fabric. The strip set will be 1½″ wide × WOF. Make 2 strip sets of each colored fabric for a total of 10 strip sets.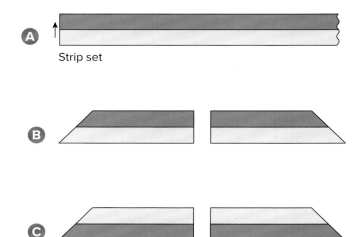

2. Sew the remaining white 1″ strips together into strip sets. Each strip set will be 1½″ wide × WOF. Press toward one side. Make 2 strip sets; you will have one strip leftover.

3. Fold each strip set in half, wrong sides together. Using the Mini Braid Template or Template J (page 126), subcut 12 braid pieces 1½″ × 4″ from each strip set. If you need a refresher, refer to Cutting the Braid Pieces (page 9).

4. From each white and color fabric strip set, you will get braids with the white fabric on the bottom of the braid piece and braids with the white fabric at the top of the braid piece. Separate the braid pieces into 2 groups: the braid pieces with the white fabric at the bottom and the braid pieces with the white fabric at the top. **B**–**C**

5. Refer to the instructions in Sewing a Basic Braid (page 11). Using the braid pieces with the white at the bottom, start with a braid piece on the right and sew 16 braid pieces together into a long braid.

6. Sew 4 white braid pieces 1½″ × 4″ to the top of the braid.

7. Cut the braid into a rectangle 3½″ × 12″. If you need guidance, refer to Trimming a Basic Braid (page 11). Make 3 braids. **D**

8. Repeat Steps 5–7, using the pieced braids with the white at the top. **E**

A Strip set

Braid with white at the top — Braid with white at the bottom

Making the Pillow Front

1. For each pillow, use the braids with the same arrangement (white at the bottom or white at the top). Refer to the pillow top assembly diagram at right. Use the 3 braids with the white at the bottom, rotate the center braid, and sew a white sashing rectangle 1¾″ × 12″ between them. Press toward the sashing.

2. Sew a white border 1¾″ × 12″ to the sides of the pillow top. Press toward the border.

3. Sew a white border 1¾″ × 14½″ to the top and bottom of the pillow top. Press toward the border. The pillow top should measure 14½″ × 14½″. **F**

4. Repeat Steps 1–3 with the 3 braids from Step 8 to create the second pillow top.

5. Layer the pillow top with the batting or fusible fleece and quilt as desired. If you're using fusible fleece, fuse the fleece to the wrong side of the pillow top, following the manufacturer's instructions. Once you have quilted your pillow top, trim the batting or fleece even with the edges of the pillow top.

Making the Pillow Back

1. Fuse interfacing to the wrong sides of each 9½″ × 14½″ back piece, following the manufacturer's instructions.

2. Place the zipper right side down, centered on one back piece. **G**

3. Stitch the zipper to the back piece with a ¼″ seam. A zipper foot may be helpful. Fold the fabric away from the zipper and topstitch on the right side of the backing fabric about ⅛″ from the folded edge. **H**

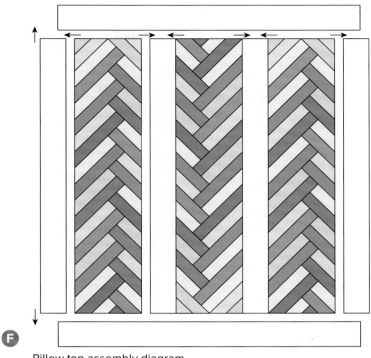

F

Pillow top assembly diagram

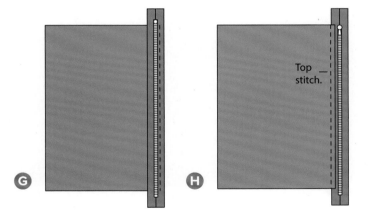

G

H

Top stitch.

4. On the other back piece, fold over a 14½″ edge about 1½″ with wrong sides together and press. Unfold and center the raw edge of the second pillow back, right side down, along the other side of the zipper and stitch in place.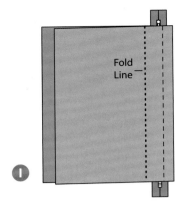

5. Refold the backing piece along the fold line you created so the fold covers the zipper and secure in place. I like to secure the sides with binding clips. Turn the entire back unit over so the back piece is **wrong** side up and topstitch along the same stitching line you just sewed.

TOPSTITCHING TIP • First, your bobbin thread will show on the outside of the back, so make sure it will look good. Second, if you accidentally sew along the wrong seam, you will sew the flap closed!

6. Turn the pillow back right side up. **Open the zipper partway** and trim the sides of the zipper even with the sides of the pillow back. Stitch across both ends of the zipper to secure it. Trim the pillow back to 14½″ × 14½″.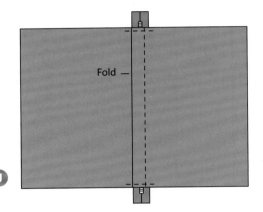

Finishing

1. Layer the pillow top **wrong sides together** with the pillow back. Match up all the sides. Optional: At this point, although you can move directly to binding the pillow, for ease in handling, you can also stitch along all 4 sides of the pillow with an ⅛″ seam.

2. Bind the pillow cover.

3. Stuff the pillow form inside the pillow cover and ta-done!

PINK IMPRESSION

Finished flower blocks: 6″ × 6″ • **Finished leaf blocks:** 6″ × 6″, 6″ × 10″
Finished quilt: 58½″ × 68½″

Pieced flower blocks are just so sweet, and making these by using a braid technique means no paper piecing!

Fabric Selection

For the flower, I wanted a medium-light and medium-dark color for the petals and a light color for the center of the flower. Using ombré fabrics meant that each flower would look slightly different, depending on which part of the ombré strip ended up in the block. It gave the quilt a very organic feel, as no two flowers are exactly alike!

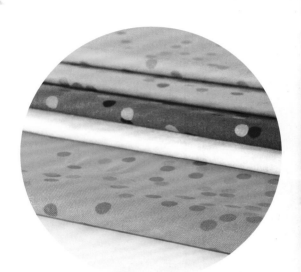

Materials

Yardages are based on 40″-wide fabric.

White background: 4½ yards

Yellow ombré: ¼ yard

Light pink ombré: ½ yard

Dark pink ombré: ⅝ yard

Green ombré: 1½ yards

Binding: ⅝ yard

Backing: 3¾ yards

Batting: 66″ × 76″

Cutting

CUTTING TIP • Pieces marked with an asterisk (*) can be cut oversized for Half-Square Triangle (HST) units.

White Background

Cut 2 strips 6½″ × WOF; subcut into 9 squares 6½″ × 6½″ and 8 rectangles 6½″ × 2½″.

Cut 3 strips 4½″ × WOF; piece strips together across short ends and subcut into 2 sashings 4½″ × 54½″.

Cut 4 strips 3½″ × WOF; piece strips together across short ends and subcut into 2 top and bottom borders 3½″ × 58½″.

Cut 4 strips 2½″ × WOF; piece strips together across short ends and subcut into 2 side borders 2½″ × 62½″ and 10 squares 2½″ × 2½″.

Cut 5 strips 2½″ × WOF; subcut into 10 rectangles 2½″ × 6½″, 26 squares 2½″ × 2½″, and 18 rectangles 2½″ × 1½″.

Cut 11 strips 1⅞″ × WOF*; subcut into 216 squares 1⅞″ × 1⅞″*.

Cut 9 strips 1½″ × WOF. Using the Braid Template or Template L (page 126), subcut 54 braid pieces 1½″ × 6½″. If you need a refresher, refer to Cutting the Braid Pieces (page 9).

Cut 30 strips 1½″ × WOF; subcut into 27 rectangles 1½″ × 3¼″, 162 rectangles 1½″ × 3″, 117 rectangles 1½″ × 2½″, and 171 squares 1½″ × 1½″.

Cut 13 strips 1″ × WOF; subcut into 36 rectangles 1″ × 10½″ and 18 rectangles 1″ × 6½″.

Cutting list continued on page 90.

MADE BY
Kate Colleran.

QUILTED BY
Lisa Soderborg of
The Quilted Cricket.

FABRICS ARE FROM
*the Best of Ombré
Confetti Metallics from
Moda Fabrics.*

Cutting list continued.

Yellow Ombré

Cut 2 strips 1½″ × WOF; subcut into 27 squares 1½″ × 1½″.

Light Pink Ombré

Cut 8 strips 1½″ × WOF; subcut into 27 rectangles 1½″ × 4¼″, 27 rectangles 1½″ × 3¾″, and 27 rectangles 1½″ × 2¾″.

Dark Pink Ombré

Cut 4 strips 1½″ × WOF; subcut into 27 rectangles 1½″ × 5¼″.

Cut 9 strip 1½″ × WOF. Using the Braid Template or Template L (page 126), subcut into 54 braid pieces 1½″ × 6½″. If you need a refresher, refer to Cutting the Braid Pieces (page 9).

Green Ombré

Cut 11 strips 1⅞″ × WOF*; subcut into 216 squares 1⅞″ × 1⅞″*.

Cut 8 strips 1½″ × WOF; subcut into 18 rectangles 1½″ × 10½″ and 9 rectangles 1½″ × 6½″.

Cut 9 strips 1½″ × WOF. Using the Braid Template or Template L (page 126), subcut into 54 braid pieces 1½″ × 6½″. If you need a refresher, refer to Cutting the Braid Pieces (page 9).

Binding

Cut 7 strips 2¼″ × WOF.

Backing

Cut 2 pieces 66″ × WOF and piece crosswise to make a backing about 66″ wide × 76″ long.

ASSEMBLY

Seam allowances are ¼″ unless otherwise noted. Follow the arrows for pressing suggestions.

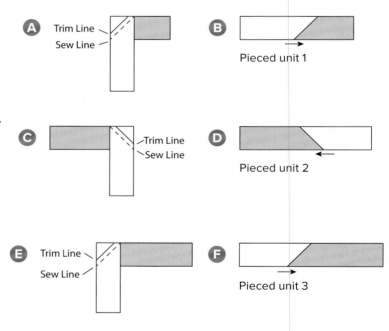

Making the Flower Braid Blocks

Before we can make our flower braid blocks, we need to piece together some strips.

Making Pieced Braid Pieces

1. Position a white rectangle 1½″ × 3¼″ right sides together (RST) on top of a light pink rectangle 1½″ × 2¾″, aligning the upper-left corners. Draw a diagonal line as shown. Stitch on the line and trim the seam to ¼″. Press toward the light pink rectangle. The pieced rectangle should measure 1½″ × 4½″. Make 27 of unit 1. **A–B**

2. Position a white rectangle 1½″ × 3″ RST on top of a light pink rectangle 1½″ × 3¾″, aligning the upper-right corners. Draw a diagonal line as shown. Stitch on the line and trim the seam to ¼″. Press toward the light pink rectangle. The pieced rectangle should measure 1½″ × 5¼″. Make 27 of unit 2. **C–D**

3. Position a white rectangle 1½″ × 3″ RST on top of a light pink rectangle 1½″ × 4¼″, aligning the upper-left corners. Draw a diagonal line as shown. Stitch on the line and trim the seam to ¼″. Press toward the light pink triangle. The pieced rectangle should measure 1½″ × 5¾″. Make 27 of unit 3. **E–F**

4. Position a white rectangle 1½″ × 2½″ RST on top of a dark pink rectangle 1½″ × 5¼″, aligning the upper-right corners. Draw a diagonal line as shown. Stitch on the line and trim the seam to ¼″. Press toward the dark pink rectangle. The pieced rectangle should measure 1½″ × 6¼″. Make 27 of unit 4. **G**–**H**

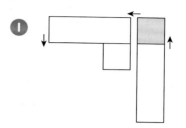

Making the Braid

1. Refer to the instructions in Sewing a Basic Braid (page 11). Start the braid by sewing a white square 1½″ × 1½″ to the bottom of a white rectangle 1½″ × 3″ along the 3″ edge. Press toward the square.

2. Sew a yellow square 1½″ × 1½″ to a white rectangle 1½″ × 3″. Press toward the square.

3. Sew the white and yellow pieced rectangle to the side of the unit from Step 1. Press toward the unit from Step 1. **I**

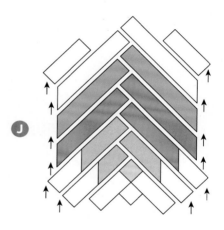

4. Sew a pieced unit 1 to the top of the braid on the left. Press toward the unit 1.

5. Sew a pieced unit 2 to the top of the braid on the right. Press toward the unit 2.

6. Sew a pieced unit 3 to the top of the braid on the left. Press toward the unit 3.

7. Sew a pieced unit 4 to the top of the braid on the right. Press toward the unit 4.

8. Sew 2 dark pink braid pieces 1½″ × 6½″ to the braid, followed by 2 green braid pieces 1½″ × 6½″ and 2 white braid pieces 1½″ × 6½″.

9. Sew a white rectangle 1½″ × 3″ to the top of the braid on both sides, near the angled end of the braid. **J**

10. Trim across the bottom of the braid, starting ¼″ below the bottom point of the light pink points. Keeping the yellow square centered in your braid when you trim the sides of the braid, cut the braid into a 6½″ × 6½″ flower-top block. Make a total of 27 flower-top blocks. **K**–**L**

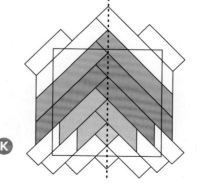

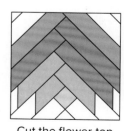

Cut the flower-top block to 6½″ × 6½″.

Making the Leaf Blocks

We will be making 2 different Leaf blocks; one block has 4 leaf units, and one block has 6 leaf units.

Making the Leaf Units

1. Make 432 HST units from 216 white squares and 216 green squares 1⅞″ × 1⅞″. Press toward the green. HST units should measure 1½″ × 1½″. If you oversized the squares, trim to size. If you need more information on making HST units, refer to How to Make Half-Square Triangle Units (page 123). **M**

2. Sew 3 HST units and a white square 1½″ × 1½″ into a Four-Patch leaf unit. Note the rotation of the HST units. Swirl the center seam. Make a total of 144 leaf units. **N**

Making the Four-Leaf Block

1. Sew a leaf unit to the top of a white 1½″ × 2½″ rectangle. Press toward the white rectangle. Note the rotation of the leaf unit. Make 2 left units.

2. Sew the 2 left units together. Make a total of 27 left leaf units. **O**

3. Sew a leaf unit to the top of a white rectangle 1½″ × 2½″. Press toward the white rectangle. Note the rotation of the leaf unit. Make 2 right units.

4. Sew the 2 right units together. Make a total of 27 right leaf units. **P**

5. Sew a left leaf unit to the left side of a green rectangle 1½″ × 6½″ and a right leaf unit to the other side. Press toward the green rectangle.

6. Sew a white rectangle 1″ × 6½″ to both sides of the block. Press toward the white rectangle. The Four-Leaf block should measure 6½″ × 6½″. Make a total of 9 Four-Leaf blocks. **Q**

M   **N** Leaf unit

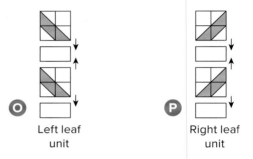

O Left leaf unit   **P** Right leaf unit

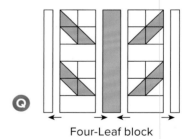

Q Four-Leaf block

Making the Six-Leaf Blocks

1. Sew a leaf unit to the bottom of a left leaf unit.

2. Sew a white square 2½″ × 2½″ to the bottom of the left leaf unit. The long left leaf unit should measure 2½″ × 10½″. Make a total of 18 long left leaf units. **R**

3. Sew a leaf unit to the bottom of a right leaf unit.

4. Sew a white square 2½″ × 2½″ to the bottom of the right leaf unit. The long right leaf unit should measure 2½″ × 10½″. Make a total of 18 long right leaf units. **S**

3. Sew a long left leaf unit to the left side of a green rectangle 1½″ × 10½″ and a long right leaf unit to the other side. Press toward the green rectangle.

4. Sew a white rectangle 1″ × 10½″ to both sides of the block. Press toward the white rectangles.

5. Sew a white rectangle 2½″ × 6½″ to the bottom of the block. Press toward the white rectangle. The six-leaf block should measure 6½″ × 12½″. Make a total of 18 Six-Leaf blocks. **T**

Making the Flower Blocks

We will make 2 different Flower blocks.

1. Sew a Six-Leaf block to the bottom of a flower-top block. Press toward the flower top. This Flower block 1 should measure 6½″ × 18½″. Make 18 of Flower block 1. **U**

2. Sew a Four-Leaf block to the bottom of a flower-top block. Press toward the flower top.

3. Sew a white 6½″ square to the bottom of the Flower block. Press toward the white square. This Flower block 2 should measure 6½″ × 18½″. Make 9 of Flower block 2. **V**

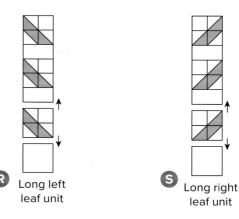

R Long left leaf unit

S Long right leaf unit

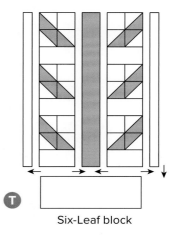

T

Six-Leaf block

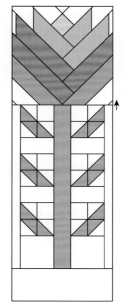

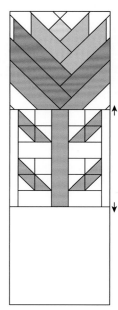

U Flower block 1

V Flower block 2

Making the Quilt

1. Referring to the quilt assembly diagram, at right, sew 6 Flower block 1 and 3 Flower block 2 in a row. Note the placement of Flower block 2 and alternate the direction of the blocks. Press the blocks toward one side. The row should measure 18½″ × 54½″. Make 3 flower rows.

2. Sew the 3 flower rows together, with a white sashing strip 4½″ × 54½″ between the rows. Press toward the sashing.

3. Sew a white border 2½″ × 62½″ to both sides of the quilt top. Press toward the borders.

4. Sew a white border 3½″ × 58½″ to the top and bottom of the quilt top. Press toward the borders. The quilt top should measure 58½″ × 66½″. Ⓦ

Finishing

1. Layer the quilt top with batting and backing and quilt as desired.

2. Bind the quilt.

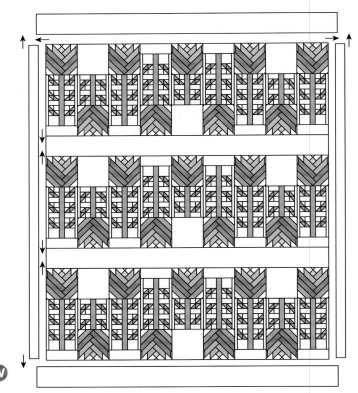

Quilt assembly diagram

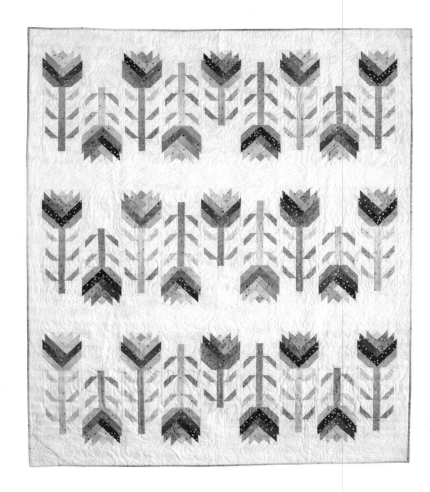

SAMPLER QUILT

Now that you have made lots of different projects, each with a different style braid, let's put them all together into one fun sampler quilt!

The *Sunny Vale* quilt has basic braids, braids with varying size strips, pieced braids, and the faux braid block. It also has two different star blocks and pinwheel blocks.

The colors and fabrics for this quilt were picked to represent a sunny garden on a warm spring day. The flowers are blooming, the grass is green, the sky is a soft blue, and the warmth of the sun feels wonderful after a long winter. Can't you just hear the birds singing? You are in botanical heaven!

As you work through the quilt, if you need more information on basic braids or varying strips, refer to the chapter for each technique.

The cutting is broken down by block; the fabric amounts reflect making the entire quilt.

SUNNY VALE

Finished quilt: 60½″ × 71″

Sampler quilts are such a fun way to try out a bunch of different blocks and different types of braids. This quilt feels like a lovely garden in the spring!

Fabric Selection

To make the quilt feel like a garden, I chose fabrics that felt light and springy: yellows, pinks, blues, and greens, with pops of orange, turquoise, and raspberry. A quilt with rows full of bright blooms, green grass, and sunshine!

Materials

Yardages are based on 40″-wide fabric.

Fabric A, turquoise: 1 yard

Fabric B, orange: ⅞ yard

Fabric C, white background: 2 yards

Fabric D, orchid pink: ⅜ yard

Fabric E, aqua: ½ yard

Fabric F, medium yellow: ⅝ yard

Fabric G, medium green: ⅜ yard

Fabric H, medium light green: ½ yard

Fabric I, light green: ⅜ yard

Fabric J, medium dark blue: ⅜ yard

Fabric K, medium dark green: ½ yard

Fabric L, light yellow: ¾ yard

Fabric M, raspberry: ⅝ yard

Fabric N, pink: ⅜ yard

Fabric O, light pink: ⅜ yard

Fabric P, yellow: ⅝ yard

Fabric Q, periwinkle blue: ⅜ yard

Fabric R, medium light blue: ½ yard

Fabric S, light blue: ⅜ yard

Binding: ⅝ yard

Backing: 4 yards

Batting: 69″ × 79″

Seam allowances are ¼″ unless otherwise noted. Follow the arrows for pressing suggestions.

If you need information on making Flying Geese (FG) units or Half-Square Triangle (HST) units, or on how to swirl the seams, refer to Basics Refresher (page 123).

CUTTING TIP • Pieces marked with an asterisk (*) can be cut oversized for HST units.

MORNING GLORY BLOCK
Finished block: 18″ × 18″

Cutting

Fabric A, Turquoise

Cut 1 strip 7¼″ × WOF*; subcut into 1 square 7¼″ × 7¼″* and 4 squares 3⅞″ × 3⅞″*.

Fabric B, Orange

Cut 1 strip 4⅞″ × WOF*; subcut into 4 squares 3⅞″ × 3⅞″*. Save the rest of the strip for the Summer Berries block.

Fabric C, White Background

Cut 1 strip 7¼″ × WOF*; subcut into 1 square 7¼″ × 7¼″* and 4 squares 3⅞″ × 3⅞″*. Save the rest of the strip for the Summer Berries block.

Cut 1 strip 3½″ × WOF; subcut into 4 squares 3½″ × 3½″. Save the rest of the strip for the Foxtrot block.

Fabric D, Orchid Pink

Cut 1 strip 4¼″ × WOF*; subcut into 4 squares 3⅞″ × 3⅞″*. Save the rest of the strip for the Pampas Plume block.

Fabric E, Aqua

Cut 1 strip 3½″ × WOF; subcut into 4 squares 3½″ × 3½″.

Fabric F, Medium Yellow

Cut 1 strip 6½″ × WOF; subcut into 1 square 6½″ × 6½″. Save the rest of the strip for the Pampas Plume block.

BLOCK ASSEMBLY

1. Make 4 FG units from 1 turquoise square 7¼″ × 7¼″ and 4 orange squares 3⅞″ × 3⅞″. Press toward the orange triangles. FG units should measure 3½″ × 6½″. If you oversized, trim to size.

2. Make 4 FG units from 1 white background square 7¼″ × 7¼″ and 4 turquoise squares 3⅞″ × 3⅞″. Press toward the turquoise triangles. FG units should measure 3½″ × 6½″. If you oversized, trim to size.

3. Make 8 HST units from 4 white and 4 orchid pink squares 3⅞″ × 3⅞″ squares. Press toward the orchid pink. HST units should measure 3½″ × 3½″. If you oversized the squares, trim to size. **C**

4. Sew a turquoise FG unit to the top of an orange FG unit. Press toward the orange FG unit. The side unit should measure 6½″ × 6½″. Make 4 side units. **D**

5. Sew 2 HST units, 1 white square 3½″ × 3½″, and 1 aqua square 3½″ × 3½″ into a Four-Patch unit. Press toward the HST units in each row and press the center seam toward the top row. The corner unit should measure 6½″ × 6½″. Make 4 corner units.

6. Refer to the block assembly diagram and sew a side unit to both sides of a medium yellow square 6½″ × 6½″. Press toward the side units. The center row should measure 6½″ × 18½″. Make 1 center row.

7. Sew a corner unit to both sides of a side unit. Note the rotation of the units. Press toward the side units. The outer row should measure 6½″ × 18½″. Make 2 outer rows.

8. Sew an outer row to the top and bottom of the center row. Swirl the seams and press flat. The Morning Glory block should measure 18½″ × 18½″. **F**

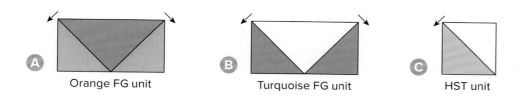

A — Orange FG unit

B — Turquoise FG unit

C — HST unit

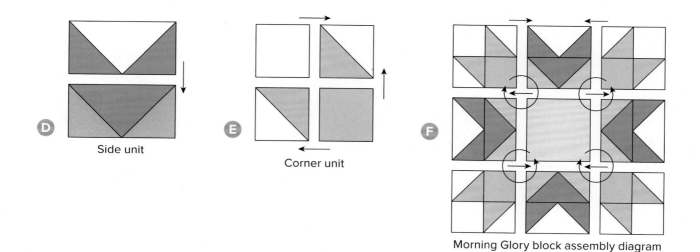

D — Side unit

E — Corner unit

F — Morning Glory block assembly diagram

HEDGEROW

Finished block: 18″ × 28″

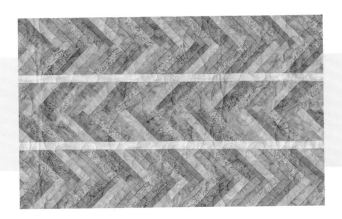

Cutting

Fabric A, Turquoise

Cut 6 strips 1¼″ by WOF. Using the Braid Template or Template H (page 125), subcut 34 braid pieces 1¼″ × 5¾″.

Fabric G, Medium Green

Cut 6 strips 1¼″ by WOF. Using the Braid Template or Template H (page 125), subcut 34 braid pieces 1¼″ × 5¾″.

Fabric H, Medium Light Green

Cut 6 strips 1¼″ by WOF. Using the Braid Template or Template H (page 125), subcut 34 braid pieces 1¼″ × 5¾″.

Fabric I, Light Green

Cut 6 strips 1¼″ by WOF. Using the Braid Template or Template H (page 125), subcut 34 braid pieces 1¼″ × 5¾″.

Fabric J, Medium Dark Blue

Cut 6 strips 1″ by WOF. Using the Braid Template or Template C (page 125), subcut 34 braid pieces 1″ × 5¾″.

Fabric K, Medium Dark Green

Cut 6 strips 1″ by WOF. Using the Braid Template or Template C (page 125), subcut 34 braid pieces 1″ × 5¾″.

Fabric L, Light Yellow

Cut 2 strips 1¼″ by WOF; subcut into 2 rectangles 1¼″ × 28½″.

ASSEMBLY

Before you start sewing the braids, you need to lay out the fabrics in a pleasing order. Remember, when adding strips of different widths, you always want to add pairs of the same width. For example, add two of the light green 1¼″-wide braid pieces, one on the left and one on the right, then add two of the medium dark green skinny 1″-wide braid pieces, then add two of the medium light green 1¼″-wide braid pieces, and so on.

Or you can mix up the colors like I did by adding a medium dark green 1″ braid piece paired with a medium dark blue 1″ braid piece and then add a medium green 1¼″-wide braid piece paired with a medium light green 1¼″-wide braid piece. Just be sure to pair by size!

1. Sew the various blue and green braid pieces together into a long braid. You will need a braid about 86″ long.

PIECING TIP • The braid pieces on the left side of the braid will all be even, while on the right side of the braid, the pieces will be jagged. Don't worry! That is how it is supposed to look.

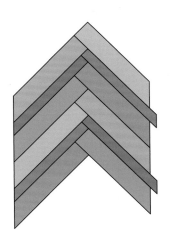

2. Trim the braid to 3 braids 6″ wide × 28½″. If you need guidance on trimming the braid, refer to How to Use Varying Size Braid Pieces (page 33).

CUTTING TIP • When making a really long braid that will be cut into smaller units, I like to cut as I go so I don't have to handle a lengthy braid piece—or in this case, a really, really long braid! Once your braid is long enough, cut off your first long braid section, then keep adding pieces to the braid until you can cut the next one, and so on!

3. Sew a light yellow rectangle 1¼″ × 28½″ between the 3 braid units. Rotate the center braid. Press toward the rectangles. The hedgerow block should measure 18½″ × 28½″.

Hedgerow block assembly

FORGET ME NOT

Finished row 1: 6″ × 18″ • **Finished row 2:** 4″ × 8½″

Cutting

CUTTING TIP • Pieces marked with an asterisk (*) can be cut oversized for Half-Square Triangle (HST) units.

Fabric A, Turquoise

Cut 1 strip 2⅞″ × WOF*; subcut into 12 squares 2⅞″ × 2⅞″*.

Fabric C, White Background

Cut 1 strip 2⅞″ × WOF*; subcut into 12 squares 2⅞″ × 2⅞″*.

Cut 1 strip 1½″ × WOF; subcut into 2 rectangles 1½″ × 18½″.

Cut 1 strip 1¼″ × WOF; subcut into 2 rectangles 1¼″ × 4½″ and 2 rectangles 1″ × 4½″.

ASSEMBLY

1. Make 24 HST units from 12 turquoise and 12 white squares 2⅞″ × 2⅞″. Press toward the turquoise. HST units should measure 2½″ × 2½″. If you oversized the squares, trim to size. **A**

2. Sew 4 HST units together into a Pinwheel block. Note the rotation of the HST units. Swirl the center seam. The Pinwheel block should measure 4½″ × 4½″. Make 6 pinwheels. **B**

3. Sew a pinwheel to the top and bottom of a white background rectangle 1″ × 4½″. Press toward the white rectangle. The unit should measure 4½″ × 9″. Make 2 units, setting 1 aside for the Forget Me Not block for row 2. **C**

4. Sew a white rectangle 1¼″ × 4½″ to the top and bottom of the other pinwheel unit from Step 3. Then, sew a pinwheel to the top and bottom of the unit. Press toward the white rectangles.

5. Sew a white rectangle 1½″ × 18½″ to both sides of the unit from Step 4. Press toward the white rectangles. The Forget Me Not block for row 1 should measure 6½″ × 18½″. **D**

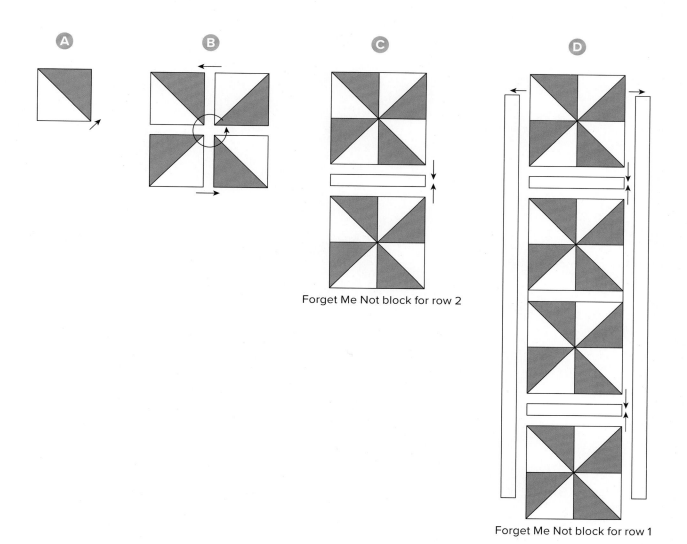

Forget Me Not block for row 2

Forget Me Not block for row 1

FOXTROT
Finished block: 6″ × 12″

Cutting

Fabric C, White Background

Subcut the leftover 3½″ × 24″ strip from the Morning Glory block into 1 strip 1½″ × 24″ and 1 strip 1⅞″* × 26″. Subcut the 1½″ strip into 8 rectangles 1½″ × 3″. Subcut the 1⅞″* strip into 12 squares 1⅞″ × 1⅞″*.

Cut 2 strips 1½″ × WOF. Using the Braid Template or Template L (page 126), subcut 4 braid pieces 1½″ × 6½″. Subcut the rest of the strips into 2 rectangles 1½″ × 3¼″, 4 rectangles 1½″ × 3″, 10 rectangles 1½″ × 2½″, and 10 squares 1½″ × 1½″.

Cut 1 strip 1″ × WOF; subcut into 4 rectangles 1″ × 6½″.

Fabric H, Medium Light Green

Cut 1 strip 1⅞″ × WOF*; subcut into 12 squares 1⅞″ × 1⅞″*.

Cut 1 strip 1½″ × WOF. Using the Braid Template or Template L (page 126), subcut 4 braid pieces 1½″ × 6½″. Subcut the rest of the strips into 2 rectangles 1½″ × 6½″.

Fabric M, Raspberry

Cut 1 strip 1½″ × WOF. Using the Braid Template or Template L (page 126), subcut 4 braid pieces 1½″ × 6½″.

Fabric N, Pink

Cut 1 strip 1½″ × WOF; subcut into 2 rectangles 1½″ × 5¼″ and 2 rectangles 1½″ × 4¼″.

Fabric O, Light Pink

Cut 1 strip 1½″ × WOF; subcut into 2 rectangles 1½″ × 3¾″ and 2 rectangles 1½″ × 2¾″.

Fabric P, Yellow

Cut 1 strip 1½″ × WOF; subcut into 2 squares 1½″ × 1½″.

BLOCK ASSEMBLY

The block is made in two parts, the flower top and the leaf unit. Let's start with the flower.

Making the Flower Braid Blocks

Before we can make our Flower Braid blocks, we need to piece together some strips.

Making Pieced Braid Pieces

1. Position a white rectangle 1½″ × 3¼″ right sides together (RST) on top of a light pink rectangle 1½″ × 2¾″, aligning the upper-left corners. Draw a diagonal line as shown. Stitch on the line and trim the seam to ¼″. Press toward the pink. The pieced rectangle should measure 1½″ × 4½″. Make 2 of unit 1. **A** – **B**

2. Position a white rectangle 1½″ × 3″ RST on top of a light pink rectangle 1½″ × 3¾″, aligning the upper-right corners. Draw a diagonal line as shown. Stitch on the line and trim the seam to ¼″. Press toward the pink. The pieced rectangle should measure 1½″ × 5¼″. Make 2 of unit 2. **C** – **D**

3. Position a white rectangle 1½″ × 3″ RST on top of a pink rectangle 1½″ × 4¼″, aligning the upper-left corners. Draw a diagonal line as shown. Stitch on the line and trim the seam to ¼″. Press toward the pink. The pieced rectangle should measure 1½″ × 5¾″. Make 2 of unit 3. **E** – **F**

4. Position a white rectangle 1½″ × 2½″ RST on top of a pink rectangle 1½″ × 5¼″, aligning the upper-right corners. Draw a diagonal line as shown. Stitch on the line and trim the seam to ¼″. Press toward the pink. The pieced rectangle should measure 1½″ × 6¼″. Make 2 of unit 4. **G** – **H**

Making the Braid

1. Sew a white square 1½″ × 1½″ to the bottom of a white rectangle 1½″ × 3″, along the 3″ edge. Press toward the square.

2. Sew a yellow square 1½″ × 1½″ to a white rectangle 1½″ × 3″. Press toward the square.

3. Sew the white and yellow pieced rectangle to the side of the unit from Step 1. Press toward the unit from Step 1. **I**

4. Refer to the braid assembly diagram and sew a pieced unit 1 to the top of the braid on the left. Press toward the unit 1.

5. Sew a pieced unit 2 to the top of the braid on the right. Press toward the unit 2.

6. Sew a pieced unit 3 to the top of the braid on the left. Press toward the unit 3.

7. Sew a pieced unit 4 to the top of the braid on the right. Press toward the unit 4.

8. Sew 2 raspberry braid pieces 1½″ × 6½″ to the braid, followed by 2 medium light green braid pieces 1½″ × 6½″ and 2 white braid pieces 1½″ × 6½″.

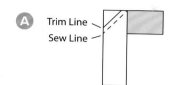
A — Trim Line / Sew Line

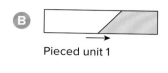
B — Pieced unit 1

C — Trim Line / Sew Line

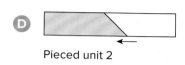
D — Pieced unit 2

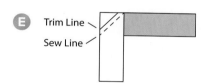
E — Trim Line / Sew Line

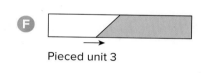
F — Pieced unit 3

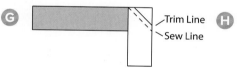
G — Trim Line / Sew Line

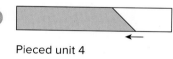
H — Pieced unit 4

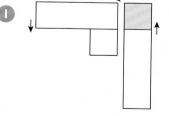
I

9. Sew a white rectangle 1½″ × 3″ to the top of the braid on both sides, near the angled end of the braid. **J**

10. Trim across the bottom of the braid, starting ¼″ below the bottom point of the light pink points. Keeping the yellow square centered in your braid when you trim the sides of the braid, cut the braid into a 6½″ × 6½″ flower-top block. Make 2 flower-top blocks. **K** – **L**

Making the Leaf Blocks

Making the Leaf Units

1. Make 24 HST units from 12 white and 12 medium light green squares 1⅞″ × 1⅞″. Press toward the green square. HST units should measure 1½″ × 1½″. If you oversized the squares, trim to size. **M**

2. Sew 3 HST units and a white square 1½″ × 1½″ into a Four-Patch unit. Note the rotation of the HST units. Swirl the center seam. Make a total of 8 leaf units. **N**

Making the Leaf Block

1. Sew a leaf unit to the top of a white rectangle 1½″ × 2½″. Press toward the white rectangle. Note the rotation of the leaf unit. Make 2 left units.

2. Sew the 2 left units together. Make a total of 2 left leaf units. **O**

3. Sew a leaf unit to the top of a white rectangle 1½″ × 2½″. Press toward the white rectangle. Note the rotation of the Four-Patch unit. Make 2 right units.

4. Sew the 2 right units together. Make a total of 2 right leaf units. **P**

5. Sew a left leaf unit to the left side of a medium light green rectangle 1½″ × 6½″ and a right leaf unit to the other side. Press toward the green rectangle.

6. Sew a white rectangle 1″ × 6½″ to both sides of the block. Press toward the white rectangles. The Leaf block should measure 6½″ × 6½″. Make 2 Four-Leaf blocks. **Q**

Making the Foxtrot Blocks

Sew a leaf block to the bottom of a flower-top block. Press toward the flower top. The Foxtrot block should measure 6½″ × 12½″. Make 2 Foxtrot blocks. **R**

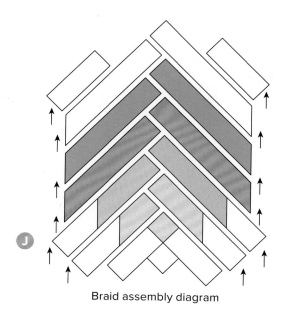

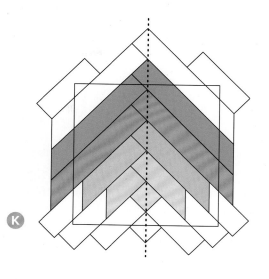

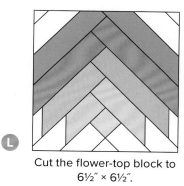

Braid assembly diagram

L

Cut the flower-top block to
6½″ × 6½″.

M

N

Leaf unit

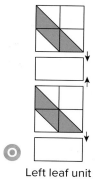

O

Left leaf unit

P

Right leaf unit

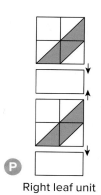

Q

Leaf block

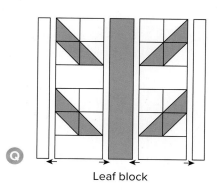

R

Foxtrot block
assembly diagram

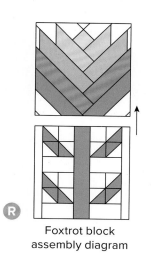

SUMMER BERRIES

Finished block: 12″ × 12″

Cutting

Fabric B, Orange

Subcut the leftover 4⅞″ × 20″ strip from the Morning Glory block into 4 squares 4⅞″ × 4⅞″*.

Fabric C, White Background

Subcut the leftover 7¼″ × 16½″ strip from the Morning Glory block into 2 squares 5¼″ × 5¼″*.

Cut 1 strip 2½″ × WOF; subcut into 16 squares 2½″ × 2½″.

Fabric D, Orchid Pink

Cut 1 strip 2½″ × WOF; subcut into 8 squares 2½″ × 2½″. Save the rest of the strip for the Hydrangea block.

Fabric M, Raspberry

Cut 1 strip 5¼″ × WOF*; subcut into 2 squares 5¼″ × 5¼″* and 2 squares 4½″ × 4½″.

Fabric Q, Periwinkle Blue

Cut 1 strip 2½″ × WOF; subcut into 8 squares 2½″ × 2½″.

BLOCK ASSEMBLY

1. Cut the 4 orange squares 4⅞″ × 4⅞″ in half on the diagonal once for 2 Half-Square Triangles (HSTs) from each square. You will have a total of 8 HSTs. **A**

2. Cut 2 white and 2 raspberry squares 5¼″ × 5¼″ in half on the diagonal twice for 4 Quarter-Square Triangles (QSTs) from each square. You will have a total of 8 QSTs from each fabric. **B** – **C**

3. Sew a white background QST to a raspberry QST along the short edges. Note the placement of each triangle. Press toward the raspberry triangles. **D**

4. Sew an orange HST to the long edge of the unit from Step 3. Press toward the orange triangle. The side unit should measure 4½″ × 4½″. If you oversized your squares, trim to size. Make a total of 8 side units. **E**

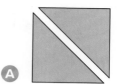

A

5. Sew 2 white, 1 orchid pink, and 1 periwinkle blue squares 2½″ × 2½″ into a Four-Patch block. Note the placement of the fabrics. Swirl the center seam. The corner unit should measure 4½″ × 4½″. Make a total of 8 corner units. **F**

6. Refer to the block assembly diagram and sew a side unit to both sides of a raspberry square 4½″ × 4½″. Press toward the raspberry square. The center row should measure 4½″ × 12½″. Make 2 center rows.

7. Sew a corner unit to both sides of a side unit. Note the rotation of both units. Press toward the corner unit. The outer row should measure 4½″ × 12½″. Make 4 outer rows.

8. Sew an outer row to the top and bottom of a center row. Swirl the seams and press flat. The Summer Berries block should measure 12½″ × 12½″. Make 2 blocks. **G**

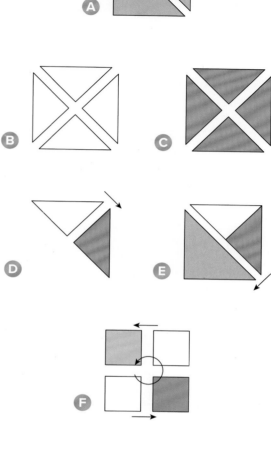

B C

D E

F

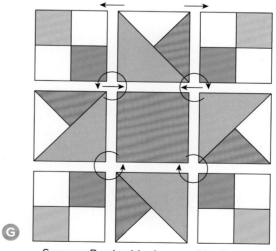

G

Summer Berries block assembly diagram

CANDY TUFT

Finished braid block 1: 6″ × 20″
Finished braid block 2: 6″ × 36″

Cutting

Fabric B, Orange

Cut 1 strip 1½″ × WOF; subcut into 9 rectangles 1½″ × 3½″.

Fabric C, White Background

Cut 11 strips 1½″ × WOF; subcut into 10 rectangles 1½″ × 6½″, 10 rectangles 1½″ × 5¾″, 75 rectangles 1½″ × 3½″, and 3 squares 1½″ × 1½″.

Fabric I, Light Green

Cut 1 strip 1½″ × WOF; subcut into 9 rectangles 1½″ × 2¾″.

Fabric J, Medium Dark Blue

Cut 1 strip 1½″ × WOF; subcut into 9 rectangles 1½″ × 3½″.

Fabric K, Medium Dark Green

Cut 1 strip 1½″ × WOF; subcut into 9 rectangles 1½″ × 3½″.

Fabric M, Raspberry

Cut 1 strip 1½″ × WOF; subcut into 9 rectangles 1½″ × 3½″.

Fabric N, Pink

Cut 1 strip 1½″ × WOF; subcut into 9 rectangles 1½″ × 2¾″.

Fabric P, Yellow

Cut 1 strip 1½″ × WOF; subcut into 9 rectangles 1½″ × 2¾″.

Fabric R, Medium Light Blue

Cut 1 strip 1½″ × WOF; subcut into 9 rectangles 1½″ × 2¾″.

BLOCK ASSEMBLY

Before we can make our braid blocks, we need to make some pieced units.

Making Pieced Units

1. Sew a white rectangle 1½″ × 3½″ to the 9 orange, medium dark blue, medium dark green, and raspberry rectangles 1½″ × 3½″. Press toward the colored fabric. Dark units should measure 1½″ × 6½″. **A**

2. Sew a white rectangle 1½″ × 3½″ to the 9 light green, pink, yellow, and medium light blue rectangles 1½″ × 2¾″. Press toward the colored fabric. Light units should measure 1½″ × 5¾″. **B**

3. To start the braid, sew a white square 1½″ × 1½″ to the bottom of a white rectangle 1½″ × 3½″, along the 3½″ edge. Press toward the square.

4. Sew a white rectangle 1½″ × 5¾″ to the top of the braid on the right. Press toward the white rectangle.

5. Sew a white rectangle 1½″ × 6½″ to the top of the braid on the left. Press toward the white rectangle.

6. Sew a pink light unit to the top of the braid on the right. Press toward the pink unit.

7. Sew a raspberry dark unit to the top of the braid on the left. Press toward the raspberry unit.

8. Continue to add the light units to the right side of the braid and the dark units to the left side of the braid. Add a total of 12 light and 12 dark units. End with 3 white rectangles 1½″ × 5¾″ on the right and 3 white rectangles 1½″ × 6½″ on the left.

9. Keeping the top of the points centered in the braid, trim the braid to 6½″ × 20½″ for the Candy Tuft block 1. The top trim should be about 1″ beyond the top point of the medium dark blue braid piece.

10. Repeat Steps 3–8, but add only 2 white right and left rectangles at the end of the braid. Make 2 braids.

11. Keeping the top of the points centered in the braid, trim the braids to 6½″ × 18½″. The top trim should be about ½″ beyond the top point of the medium dark green braid piece. **E**

12. Sew the 2 braid sections together by the top edges. Press the seam to one side. The Candy Tuft block 2 should measure 6½″ × 36½″. **F**

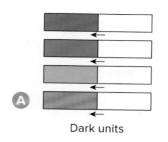

Dark units

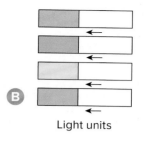

Light units

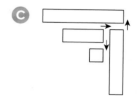

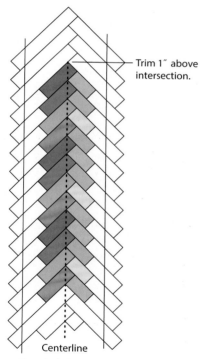

Trim 1″ above intersection.

Centerline

Candy tuft block 1 assembly diagram

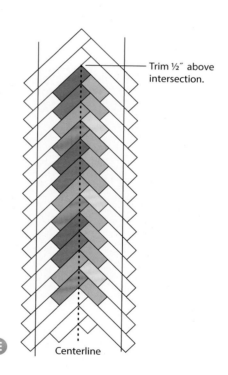

Trim ½″ above intersection.

Centerline

Candy Tuft block 2 assembly diagram

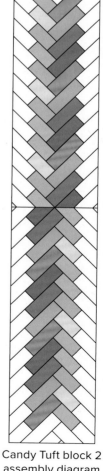

PAMPAS PLUME

Finished block: 24″ × 28″

Cutting

*CUTTING TIP • Pieces marked with * can be cut oversized for Half-Square Triangles (HST) units.*

Fabric B, Orange

Cut 3 strips 1½″ × WOF. Using the Braid Template or Template K (page 126), subcut 20 braid pieces 1½″ × 5¾″.

Fabric D, Orchid Pink

Subcut the leftover 4¼″ × 24″ strip from the Morning Glory block into 2 squares 4¼″ × 4¼″*.

Fabric F, Medium Yellow

Subcut the leftover 6½″ × 33½″ strip from the Morning Glory block into 4 strips 1½″ × 33½″. Using the Braid Template or Template K (page 126), subcut 20 braid pieces 1½″ × 5¾″.

Fabric K, Medium Dark Green

Cut 1 strip 4½″ × WOF*; subcut into 1 square 4¼″ × 4¼″*, subcut the rest of the strip into 3 strips 1½″ × 31″ and then subcut ino 50 squares 1½″ × 1½″.

Fabric L, Light Yellow

Cut 1 strip 4¼″ × WOF*; subcut into 4 squares 4¼″ × 4¼″* and 12 squares 2″ × 2″.

Cut 3 strips 1½″ × WOF. Using the Braid Template or Template K (page 126), subcut 20 braid pieces 1½″ × 5¾″.

Fabric M, Raspberry

Cut 1 strip 2⅜″ × WOF*; subcut into 12 squares 2⅜″ × 2⅜″*.

Cut 2 strips 1½″ × WOF. Using the Braid Template or Template K (page 126), subcut 16 braid pieces 1½″ × 5¾″.

Fabric N, Pink

Cut 3 strips 1½″ × WOF. Using the Braid Template or Template K (page 126), subcut 20 braid pieces 1½″ × 5¾″.

Fabric O, Light Pink

Cut 2 strips 2½″ × WOF; subcut into 2 rectangles 2½″ × 28½″. Save the rest of the strips for the Hydrangea block.

Cut 2 strips 1½″ × WOF; subcut into 2 rectangles 1½″ × 28½″.

Fabric P, Yellow

Cut 3 strips 1½″ × WOF. Using the Braid Template or Template K (page 126), subcut 20 braid pieces 1½″ × 5¾″.

BLOCK ASSEMBLY

For this block, we are making four braids and three stars. Let's start with the stars.

Making the Star Blocks

1. Make 4 HST units from 2 light yellow and 2 orchid pink squares 4¼″ × 4¼″. Press toward the orchid pink. **Do not trim!**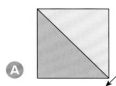

2. Draw a diagonal line corner to corner on the wrong side of 2 HST units. Layer 2 HST units right sides together (RST), nesting seams with opposite fabrics on top of one another. Sew ¼″ from the line on both sides. Cut along the diagonal line. Swirl the seams and press flat. Quarter-Square Triangle (QST) units should measure 3½″ × 3½″. If you oversized the squares, trim to size. Make 4 center QST units. You will need only 3 of them.

3. Make 8 Flying Geese (FG) units from 2 light yellow 4¼″ squares and 8 raspberry 2⅜″ squares. FG units should measure 2″ × 3½″. If you oversized, trim to size.

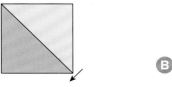

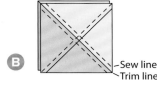
Sew line
Trim line

Center QST unit

Yellow FG unit

Green FG unit

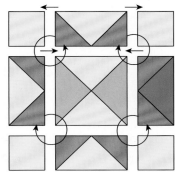
Star block 1 assembly diagram

4. Make 4 FG units from 1 medium dark green square 4¼″ × 4¼″ and 4 raspberry squares 2⅜″ × 2⅜″. FG units should measure 2″ × 3½″. If you oversized, trim to size.

5. Refer to the Star block 1 assembly diagram. Sew a yellow FG unit to the left side of a center QST unit and a green FG unit to the right side. Note the rotation of the units. Press toward the QST unit. The center row should measure 3½″ × 6½″. Make 2 center rows.

6. Sew a light yellow square 2″ × 2″ to both sides of a yellow FG unit. Press toward the squares. The outside row should measure 2″ × 3½″. Make 4 outer rows.

7. Sew an outer row to the top and bottom of a center row. Swirl the seams and press flat. The Star block 1 should measure 6½″ × 6½″. Make 2 of Star block 1.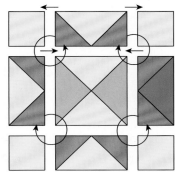

8. Refer to the Star block 2 assembly diagram (page 115). Sew a green FG unit to both sides of a center QST unit. Note the rotation of the units. Press toward the QST unit. The center row should measure 3½″ × 6½″. Make 1 center row.

9. Sew a light yellow square 2″ × 2″ to both sides of a yellow FG unit. Press toward the squares. The outside row should measure 2″ × 3½″. Make 2 outer rows.

10. Sew an outer row to the top and bottom of a center row. Swirl the seams and press flat. The Star block 2 should measure 6½″ × 6½″. Make 1 of Star block 2. **G**

Making the Braids

We will make two long braids and two short braids.

1. Sew a medium dark green square 1½″ × 1½″ to the 56 left-side braid pieces. Press toward the braid pieces. **H**

2. Lay out your braid pieces in a pleasing order. For the long braids, you will use 19 pairs of braid pieces in each braid. I added my pieces as pairs of the same color, and because I wanted my braid to end with light yellow, I also started with light yellow.

3. To start a long braid, sew a medium dark green square 1½″ × 1½″ to a right light yellow braid piece. Press toward the yellow braid piece.

4. Sew a left light yellow braid piece with a green square to the top of the braid on the left. Press toward the left-side braid piece.

5. Sew an orange braid piece to the top of the braid on the right and then an orange braid piece with a green square to the top of the braid piece on the left. Press toward the piece just added. Continue to add a total of 18 pairs of braid pieces with green squares. Sew a light yellow braid pair to the top of the braid. **I**

6. Starting at the bottom, trim the braid ¼″ below the bottom point of the second green square. Keeping the top point of the green squares centered in the braid, trim the braid to 6½″ × 22½″. Make 2 long braids. **J**

7. For the short braids, follow Steps 3–6, using 10 pairs of braid pieces with green squares. So that my braids would end with a light yellow pair, I started with a pink pair of braid pieces. Sew a light yellow braid pair to the top of the braid. Trim the braid to 6½″ × 11½″. Make 2 short braids. **K**

Making the Block

1. Refer to the block assembly diagram, at right. Sew a Star block 1 to the end of a long braid. Note the rotation of the Star block; the green FG unit should be next to the braid. Press toward the Star block. The outer row should measure 6½″ × 28½″. Make 2 outer rows.

2. Sew a short braid to both sides of the Star block 2. Note the rotation of the braids and the Star block. Press toward the Star block. The center row should measure 6½″ × 28½″. Make 1 center row.

3. Sew a light pink rectangle 1½″ × 28½″ to the top and bottom of the center row. Press toward the light pink rectangle.

4. Sew an outer braid row to the top and bottom of the center unit. Press toward the light pink rectangles.

5. Sew a light pink rectangle 2½″ × 28½″ to the top and bottom of the block. Press toward the light pink rectangle. The Pampas Plume block should measure 24½″ × 28½″. **L**

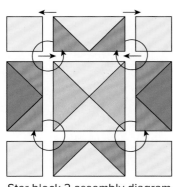

G Star block 2 assembly diagram

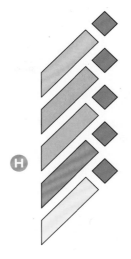

H

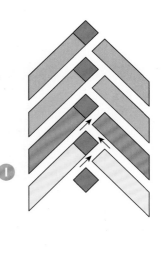

I

J

Trim ¼″ above intersection.

Trim ¼″ below intersection.

Trim to 6½″ × 22½″.

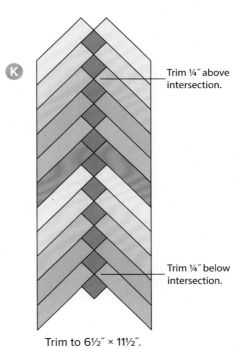

K

Trim ¼″ above intersection.

Trim ¼″ below intersection.

Trim to 6½″ × 11½″.

L Pampas Plume block assembly diagram

HYDRANGEA

Finished block: 24″ × 24″

Cutting

Fabric A, Turquoise

Cut 2 strips 2½″ × WOF; subcut into 32 squares 2½″ × 2½″.

Fabric C, White Background

Cut 3 strips 2½″ × WOF; subcut into 8 rectangles 2½″ × 8½″ and 8 rectangles 2½″ × 4½″.

Cut 1 strip 4½″ × WOF; subcut into 8 squares 4½″ × 4½″.

Fabric D, Orchid Pink

Cut 1 strip 2½″ × WOF; subcut it and the leftover 2½″ × 20″ strip from the Summer Berries block into 8 rectangles 2½″ × 6½″.

Fabric O, Light Pink

Subcut the 2 leftover 2½″ × 11½″ strips from the Pampas Plume block into 8 squares 2½″ × 2½″.

Fabric Q, Periwinkle Blue

Cut 3 strips 2½″ × WOF; subcut into 8 rectangles 2½″ × 10½″.

BLOCK ASSEMBLY

We will make 4 small blocks and sew them together into the Hydrangea block.

Making the Small Blocks

1. Sew 2 turquoise and 2 light pink squares 2½″ × 2½″ together into a Four-Patch unit. Press toward the turquoise squares, swirl the center seam, and press flat. Make 4 Four-Patch units. (A)

2. Sew a white rectangle 2½″ × 4½″ to the right edge of the Four-Patch unit. Press toward the white rectangle.

3. Sew a turquoise square 2½″ × 2½″ to a white rectangle 2½″ × 4½″. Press toward the white rectangle.

4. Sew the unit from Step 3 to the top of the Four-Patch unit. Swirl the center seam and press flat. (B)

5. Sew an orchid pink rectangle 2½″ × 6½″ to the right edge of the block. Press toward the orchid pink rectangle.

6. Sew a turquoise square 2½″ × 2½″ to an orchid pink rectangle 2½″ × 6½″. Press toward the orchid pink rectangle.

7. Sew the unit from Step 6 to the top of the block. Swirl the center seam and press flat.

8. Sew a white rectangle 2½″ × 8½″ to the right edge of the block. Press toward the white rectangle.

9. Sew a turquoise square 2½″ × 2½″ to a white rectangle 2½″ × 8½″. Press toward the white rectangle.

10. Sew the unit from Step 9 to the top of the block. Swirl the center seam and press flat.

11. Sew a periwinkle blue rectangle 2½″ × 10½″ to the right edge of the block. Press toward the periwinkle blue rectangle.

12. Sew a turquoise square 2½″ × 2½″ to a periwinkle blue rectangle 2½″ × 10½″. Press toward the periwinkle blue rectangle.

13. Sew the unit from Step 12 to the top of the block. Swirl the center seam and press flat. The unit should measure 12½″ × 12½″. **C**

14. Draw a diagonal line corner to corner on the wrong side of 2 white squares 4½″ × 4½″.

15. Position the white square in the upper-left corner of the block. Sew on the line and trim the seam to ¼″. Press toward the white triangle. **D**

16. Draw a diagonal line corner to corner on the wrong side of 2 turquoise squares 2½″ × 2½″.

17. Position the turquoise square in the upper-left corner of the block on top of the white triangle. Sew on the line and trim the seam to ¼″. Press toward the turquoise triangle. **E**

18. Repeat Steps 15 and 17 in the lower-right corner. The small block should measure 12½″ × 12½″. Make 4 small blocks. **F**

Making the Block

1. Refer to the Hydrangea block assembly diagram and sew 2 blocks together. Note the rotation of the blocks. Press toward one side. Make 2 rows.

2. Sew the 2 rows together, swirl the center seam, and press flat. The Hydrangea block should measure 24½″ × 24½″. **G**

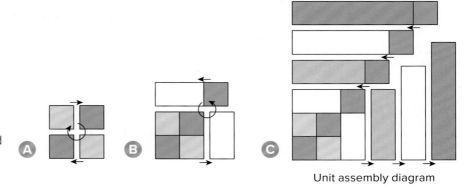

Unit assembly diagram

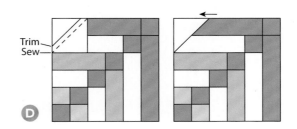

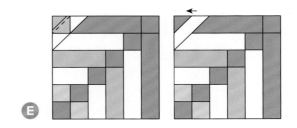

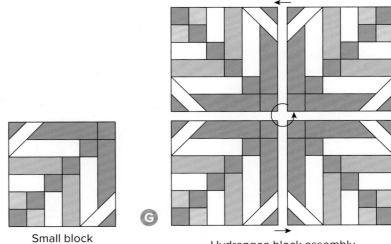

Small block

Hydrangea block assembly

SUNNY VALE

117

SKY FLOWER

Finished side border size: 4″ × 69½″
Finished top and bottom border size: 4″ × 52″

Cutting

We will be cutting the braid pieces with the fabric as a single layer. The turquoise and blue fabrics will be cut as left braid pieces, and the orange and yellow fabrics will be cut as right braid pieces.

Fabric A, Turquoise

Cut 7 strips 1¼″ × WOF. With the strip open to a single layer and the **wrong** side up, using the Braid Template or Template G (page 125), subcut 63 braid **left** pieces 1¼″ × 4½″.

CUTTING TIP • The Mini Braid template is only 4″ long. A trick to cutting braid pieces that are ½″ longer than the template is to lay the template down on the strip, line up the straight edges, and make a tiny mark in the seam allowance at the end point of the template. Move the template over to line up the 3½″ angled line with your mark. Cut along the angle edge.

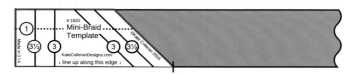

To cut the next piece, rotate the template, make a tiny mark in the seam allowance at the straight end of the template, and move the template over to line up the 3½″ straight line with your mark. Cut along the straight edge.

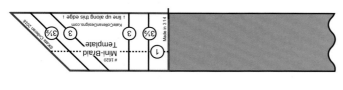

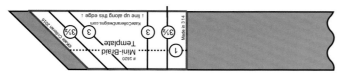

Fabric B, Orange

Cut 7 strips 1¼˝ × WOF. With the strip open to a single layer and the **right** side up, using the Braid Template or Template G (page 125), subcut 63 braid **right** pieces 1¼˝ × 4½˝.

Fabric E, Aqua

Cut 7 strips 1¼˝ × WOF. With the strip open to a single layer and the **wrong** side up, using the Braid Template or Template G (page 125), subcut 63 braid **left** pieces 1¼˝ × 4½˝.

Fabric F, Medium Yellow

Cut 7 strips 1¼˝ × WOF. With the strip open to a single layer and the **right** side up, using the Braid Template or Template G (page 125), subcut 63 braid **right** pieces 1¼˝ × 4½˝.

Fabric L, Light Yellow

Cut 7 strips 1¼˝ × WOF. With the strip open to a single layer and the **right** side up, using the Braid Template or Template G (page 125), subcut 63 braid **right** pieces 1¼˝ × 4½˝.

Fabric P, Yellow

Cut 7 strips 1¼˝ × WOF. With the strip open to a single layer and the **right** side up, using the Braid Template or Template G (page 125), subcut 63 braid **right** pieces 1¼˝ × 4½˝.

Fabric R, Medium Light Blue

Cut 7 strips 1¼˝ × WOF. With the strip open to a single layer and the **wrong** side up, using the Braid Template or Template G (page 125), subcut 63 braid **left** pieces 1¼˝ × 4½˝.

Fabric S, Light Blue

Cut 7 strips 1¼˝ × WOF. With the strip open to a single layer and the **wrong** side up, using the Braid Template or Template G (page 125), subcut 63 braid **left** pieces 1¼˝ × 4½˝.

BRAID ASSEMBLY

1. Arrange your strips into left turquoise and blue pieces and right orange and yellow pieces and craft a pleasing order. Sew the 2 color groups together into a long braid. The blue braid pieces will be on the left, and the orange and yellow braid pieces will be on the right.

2. Trim into 2 long braids 4½˝ × 71˝ and 2 short braids 4½˝ × 52½˝.

Sky Flower border block

CUTTING TIP • When making a really long braid that will be cut into smaller units, I like to cut as I go so I don't have to handle a lengthy braid piece—or in this case, a really, really long braid! Once your braid is long enough, cut off your first long braid, then keep adding pieces to the braid until you can cut the next one, and so on!

SETTING

The quilt will be sewn together in 3 rows.

Cutting

White Background

Cut 2 strips 2½″ × WOF; subcut into 6 rectangles 2½″ × 12½″.

Cut 3 strips 1¾″ × WOF; subcut into 2 rectangles 1¾″ × 32½″ and 2 rectangles 1¾″ × 16½″.

Binding

Cut 8 strips 2¼″ × WOF.

Backing

Cut 2 pieces 69″ × WOF and piece crosswise to make a backing about 69″ wide × 79″ long.

MAKING ROW 1

1. Refer to the row 1 assembly diagram and sew a Morning Glory block to the left side of the 6½″ × 18½″ Forget Me Not block. Press toward the Forget Me Not block.

2. Sew the Hedgerow block to the other side of the Forget Me Not block. Press toward the Forget Me Not block. Row 1 should measure 18½″ × 52½″. **A**

MAKING ROW 2

1. Sew a white rectangle 2½″ × 12½″ between the 2 Foxtrot blocks. Sew a white rectangle 2½″ × 12½″ to both sides of the unit. Press toward the white rectangles.

2. Sew a Summer Berries block to the right side of the unit from Step 1. Sew a white rectangle 2½″ × 12½″ to the right side of the unit. Press toward the white rectangle.

3. Sew a white rectangle 1¾″ × 32½″ to the top and bottom of the unit. Press toward the white rectangle. Unit 1 should measure 15″ × 32½″.

4. Sew a white rectangle 2½″ × 12½″ to the sides of the other Summer Berries block. Press toward the white rectangles.

5. Sew a white rectangle 1¾″ × 16½″ rectangle to the top and bottom of the Summer Berries block. Press toward the white rectangles. Unit 2 should measure 15″ × 16½″. **C**

6. Refer to the row 2 assembly diagram and sew seam 1, a partial seam joining unit 2 to the top-right edge of the 4½″ × 9″ Forget Me Not block. Press toward unit 2.

7. Sew seam 2, joining the 6½″ × 20½″ Candy Tuft block 1 to the top of the partially joined pieces. Press toward unit 2.

8. Sew seam 3, joining unit 1 to the left side of the row. Press toward unit 1.

9. Sew seam 4, joining the 6½″ × 36½″ Candy Tuft block 2 to the bottom of unit 1 and the Forgot Me Not row. Press toward unit 1.

10. Finish sewing the rest of the first partial seam, seam 5. Press toward unit 1. Row 2 should measure 21″ × 52½″.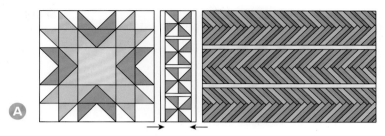

MAKING ROW 3

Sew the Pampas Plume block to the Hydrangea block. Press toward the Hydrangea block. Row 3 should measure 24½″ × 52½″. **E**

MAKING THE QUILT

1. Refer to the quilt assembly diagram (page 122) and sew the 3 rows together. Press toward row 2.

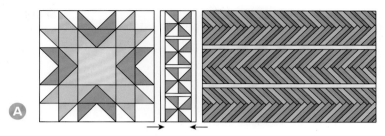

Row 1 assembly diagram

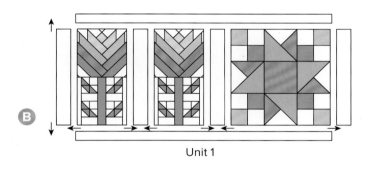

Unit 1

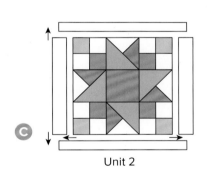

Unit 2

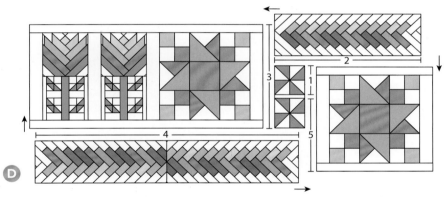

Row 2 assembly diagram

Row 3 assembly diagram

2. Sew a Sky Flower 4½″ × 52½″ braid to the top and bottom of the rows. Press toward the braid.

3. Sew a Sky Flower 4½″ × 71″ braid to both sides of the quilt top. Press toward the braid. The quilt top should measure 60½″ × 71″. **F**

FINISHING

1. Layer the quilt top with batting and backing and quilt as desired.

2. Bind the quilt.

F

Quilt assembly diagram

Basics Refresher

In quilting, there are many different ways to make the same unit. This section includes a refresher on how to make Half Square Triangle (HST) units and Flying Geese (FG) units and how to swirl the seams, just in case you need them! Feel free to use your own favorite method, but be sure to adjust the cutting in each project to reflect your method.

HOW TO MAKE HALF-SQUARE TRIANGLE UNITS

I prefer to make HST units by using the two-at-once method. Refer to the project instructions for the size of the squares.

CUTTING TIP • I like to cut my squares slightly oversized and trim my HST units to size. If you want to oversize, add ⅛″ to ¼″ to the strip and square size mentioned in the project. In each project, I have marked the strips and squares that can be oversized with an asterisk (*).

1. Draw a diagonal line corner to corner on the wrong side of the lighter square. Layer the 2 squares right sides together (RST). **A**

2. Sew ¼″ from the diagonal line on both sides. **B**

3. Cut along the diagonal line. **C**

4. Press toward the darker fabric. You will have 2 HST units. If you oversized, trim to size.

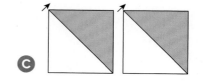

HOW TO MAKE FLYING GEESE UNITS

I like to make FG units by using the no-waste/four-at-once method. Refer to the project instructions for the size of the squares.

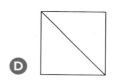

CUTTING TIP • I like to cut my squares slightly oversized and trim my FG units to size. If you want to oversize, add ⅛″ to ¼″ to the strip and square size mentioned in the project. In each project, I have marked the strips and squares that can be oversized with an asterisk (*).

1. Draw a diagonal line corner to corner across all the side squares. **D**

2. Layer the larger fabric square (the geese) with 2 side squares as shown. Sew ¼″ from the diagonal line on both sides. **E**

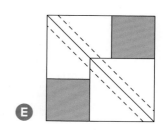

PIECING TIP • If you oversize the squares, nudge the side squares in just a few threads from the edge of the geese square rather than lining up the raw edges.

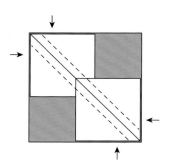

3. Cut along the diagonal line. Press toward the small triangles. **F**–**G**

4. Using one section, layer a side square as shown. Sew away from the diagonal line on both sides. **H**

5. Cut along the diagonal line. Press toward the small triangles. **I**

6. Repeat with the second section. If you oversized, trim the unit to size. You will have 4 FG units. **J**

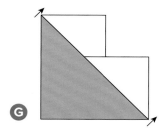

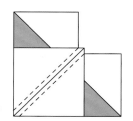

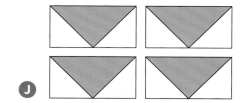

HOW TO SWIRL THE SEAMS

This pressing technique can be used when making any block where four seams come together in the middle, such as a Four-Patch. Rotating the direction you press the seams helps the block lay flat. You can even use this technique when sewing 4 blocks together.

1. Sew the 2 sets of pieces together and press with opposing seams. **K**

2. Layer the 2 units RST and sew together. Remove the couple of stitches in the center seam allowance. **L**

3. Lay the block right sides down and rotate the seam allowances. You will see a little Four-Patch in the center of the seam. Press flat. **M**

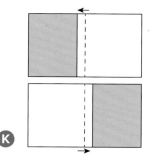

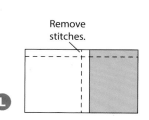

Remove stitches.

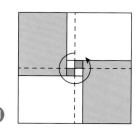

Templates

TEMPLATE A

Template A
¾" × 3"

TEMPLATES B, C, AND D

Template B
1" × 3"

Template C
1" × 5¾"

Template D
1" × 6½"

TEMPLATES E AND F

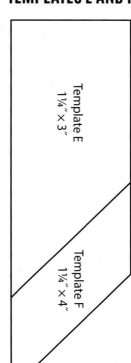

Template E
1¼" × 3"

Template F
1¼" × 4"

TEMPLATES G, H, AND I

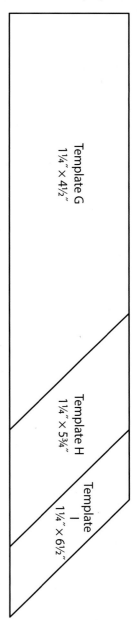

Template G
1¼" × 4½"

Template H
1¼" × 5¾"

Template I
1¼" × 6½"

TEMPLATES J, K, AND L

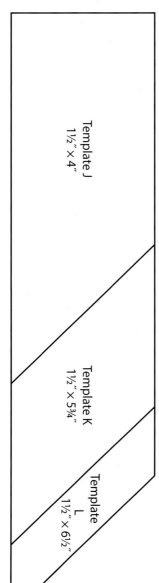

Template J
1½" × 4"

Template K
1½" × 5¾"

Template L
1½" × 6½"

TEMPLATE M

Template M
1¾" × 6¼"

TEMPLATES N AND O

TEMPLATE P

Template N
1¾" × 6½"

Template O
1¾" × 7½"

Template P
2" × 7¾"

About the Author

KATE COLLERAN is a fabric and quilt pattern designer, quilt teacher, and author. She has had quilts in many quilt magazines, has online classes on both Craftsy and Quilting Daily, and been a guest on *Fons and Porter's Love of Quilting* and *The Quilt Show* with Alex Anderson and Ricky Tims. She has taught at local quilt shops, for quilt guilds, and at national quilt shows. Her quilt patterns are known for their complete, easy-to-follow instructions with a design style inspired by traditional elements and put together with a modern twist. She is the designer of the popular Braid and Mini Braid Templates and co-author of the book *Smash Your Precut Stash*. In 2022, she started designing fabric with Island Batik. Her goal is to help quilters make a quilt by finding the methods and techniques that work for them!

Kate currently lives in Milford, Connecticut, with her husband, Jim, and her three quilt "helpers": a dog, Kira, and two cats, Lark and Luna. She enjoys spending her free time wandering about in nature.

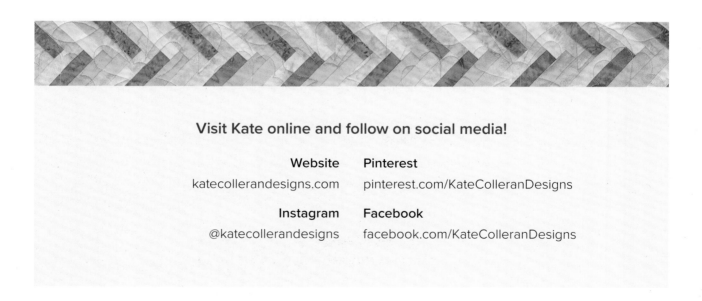

Visit Kate online and follow on social media!

Website
katecollerandesigns.com

Pinterest
pinterest.com/KateColleranDesigns

Instagram
@katecollerandesigns

Facebook
facebook.com/KateColleranDesigns